South America

FLAGS

The new compact study guide and identifier

Eve Devereux

A QUINTET BOOK

Published by The Apple Press
6 Blundell Street
London N7 9BH

Copyright © 1994 Quintet Publishing Limited.
All rights reserved. No part of this publication may be
reproduced, stored in a retrieval system or
transmitted in any form or by any means,
electronic, mechanical, photocopying, recording or
otherwise, without the permission of the copyright
holder.

ISBN 1-85076-484-0

This book was designed and produced by
Quintet Publishing Limited
6 Blundell Street
London N7 9BH

Creative Director: Richard Dewing
Designer: Bob Mathias
Senior Editor: Laura Sandelson
Editor: Del Tucker

Typeset in Great Britain by
Central Southern Typesetters, Eastbourne
Manufacturing in Singapore by Eray Scan Pte. Ltd
Printed in Singapore by Star Standard Industries Pte. Ltd

CONTENTS

INTRODUCTION	7	CENTRAL AFRICAN REPUBLIC	21	GHANA	31
AFGHANISTAN	8	CHAD	21	GREECE	31
ALBANIA	8	CHILE	21	GRENADA	32
ALGERIA	8	CHINA	22	GUATEMALA	32
ANDORRA	9	COLOMBIA	22	GUINEA	32
ANGOLA	9	COMORES	22	GUINEA-BISSAU	33
ANTARCTICA	9	CONGO	23	GUYANA	33
ANTIGUA AND BARBUDA	10	COSTA RICA	23	HAITI	33
ARGENTINA	10	CROATIA	23	HONDURAS	34
ARMENIA	10	CUBA	24	HUNGARY	34
AUSTRALIA	11	CYPRUS	24	ICELAND	34
Christmas Island		CZECH REPUBLIC	24	INDIA	35
Cocos Island		DENMARK	25	INDONESIA	35
Coral Sea Islands Territory		Faeroe Islands		IRAN	35
Norfolk Island		Greenland		IRAQ	36
AUSTRIA	12	DJIBOUTI	25	IRISH REPUBLIC	36
AZERBAIJAN	12	DOMINICA	26	ISRAEL	36
BAHAMAS	12	DOMINICAN REPUBLIC	26	ITALY	37
BAHRAIN	13	ECUADOR	26	IVORY COAST	37
BANGLADESH	13	EGYPT	27	JAMAICA	37
BARBADOS	13	EL SALVADOR	27	JAPAN	38
BELARUS	14	EQUATORIAL GUINEA	27	JORDAN	38
BELGIUM	14	ESTONIA	28	KAZAKHSTAN	38
BELIZE	14	ETHIOPIA	28	KENYA	39
BENIN	15	FIJI	28	KIRIBATI	39
BHUTAN	15	FINLAND	29	KOREA (NORTH)	39
BOLIVIA	15	FRANCE	29	KOREA (SOUTH)	40
BOSNIA AND HERZEGOVINA	16	French Guiana		KUWAIT	40
BOTSWANA	16	French Polynesia		LAOS	41
BRAZIL	16	Guadeloupe and dependencies		LATVIA	41
BRUNEI	17	Martinique		LEBANON	41
BULGARIA	17	New Caledonia		LESOTHO	42
BURKINA FASO	17	Reunion		LIBERIA	42
BURMA	18	Saint Pierre et Miquelon		LIBYA	42
BURUNDI	18	Wallis and Futuna Islands		LIECHTENSTEIN	43
CAMBODIA	18	GABON	30	LITHUANIA	43
CAMEROON	19	THE GAMBIA	30	LUXEMBOURG	43
CANADA	19	GEORGIA	30	MADAGASCAR	44
CAPE VERDE	20	GERMANY	31	MALAWI	44
				MALAYSIA	44
				MALDIVES	45

MALI	45	QATAR	56	UNITED ARAB EMIRATES	70
MALTA	45	ROMANIA	57	UNITED KINGDOM OF GREAT BRITAIN AND NORTHERN IRELAND	70
MARSHALL ISLANDS	46	RUSSIA	57		
		RWANDA	57		
MAURITANIA	46	ST. KITTS-NEVIS	58		
MAURITIUS	46	ST. LUCIA	58	Anguilla	
MEXICO	47	ST. VINCENT	58	Bermuda	
MICRONESIA	47	SAN MARINO	59	British Virgin Islands	
MOLDOVA	47	SAO TOME AND PRINCIPE	59	Cayman Islands	
MONACO	48			Falkland Islands	
MONGOLIA	48	SAUDI ARABIA	59	Gibraltar	
MOROCCO	48	SENEGAL	60	Hong Kong	
MOZAMBIQUE	49	SEYCHELLES	60	Montserrat	
NAMIBIA	49	SIERRE LEONE	60	Pitcairn Island	
NAURU	49	SINGAPORE	61	St Helena and dependencies	
NEPAL	50	SLOVAKIA	61		
NETHERLANDS	50	SLOVENIA	61	Turks and Caicos Islands	
Aruba		SOLOMON ISLANDS	62	UNITED STATES OF AMERICA	72
Netherlands Antilles		SOMALIA	62		
		SOUTH AFRICA	62	American Samoa	
NEW ZEALAND	51	SPAIN	63	Guam	
Cook Islands		SRI LANKA	63	Midway Island	
Niue Island		SUDAN	63	Virgin Islands of the United States	
Tokelau		SURINAM	64		
NICARAGUA	51	SWAZILAND	64	Wake Island	
NIGER	52	SWEDEN	64	URUGUAY	77
NIGERIA	52	SWITZERLAND	65	UZBEKISTAN	77
NORWAY	52	SYRIA	65	VANUATU	77
OMAN	53	TAJIKISTAN	65	VATICAN CITY STATE	78
PAKISTAN	53	TAIWAN	66	VENEZUELA	78
PANAMA	53	TANZANIA	66	VIETNAM	78
PAPUA NEW GUINEA	54	THAILAND	66	WESTERN SAMOA	79
		TOGO	67	YEMEN	79
PARAGUAY	54	TONGA	67	YUGOSLAVIA	79
PERU	54	TRINIDAD AND TOBAGO	67	ZAIRE	80
PHILIPPINES	55			ZAMBIA	80
POLAND	55	TUNISIA	68	ZIMBABWE	80
PORTUGAL	55	TURKEY	68		
Azores		TURKMENISTAN	68		
Macao		TUVALU	69		
Madeira		UGANDA	69		
PUERTO RICO	56	UKRAINE	69		

INTRODUCTION

We've a war, an' a debt, an' a flag;
an' ef this
Ain't to be inderpendunt, why,
wut on airth is?

The US poet, essayist and diplomat James Russell Lowell (1819–91) was, of course, writing ironically in *The Biglow Papers*, his epic denouncing the pro-slavery party and the conduct of the government, but he touched a truth when he made his Yankee narrator include a flag among his list of essential possessions for the would-be independent nation. Since earliest times flags have been something more than functional objects, standards used for identification on the battlefield or to denote different allegiances. They early became symbols of human aspirations, loyalties, ideals, desires . . . and their modern-day national versions can still have a powerful effect even on those who would regard the sentiment of patriotism as nothing more than an expression of tunnel-vision and parochialism: it is not for nothing that in many countries there are strict penalties for the offence of defiling the flag, for in so doing the offender is also defiling the nation itself.

Every modern national, state and provincial flag has a story attached to it. Its colours may be of heraldic origin or, especially in the instances of many nations that established themselves within this past century, they may symbolize the ideals underpinning the setting up of the new nation – ideals that, sadly, are more often than not acknowledged in their violation, the flags of the most vicious and bloody tyrannies, normally being replete with colours signifying purity, democracy, peace and goodwill. The emblems, too, generally have a significance beyond the historical, although some can be traced back for a millennium or more. In this book I have done my best to explain the symbolism of approximately two hundred flags and, where relevant, to tell the often fascinating stories that lie behind their modern appearance.

Since this is a book for the lay reader, terminology that might not be immediately comprehensible to such a reader has been shunned. My apologies to heraldic purists.

The few months prior to this edition going to press have continued to be turbulent in terms of the world's political geography. The most recent changes having taken place in Eastern Europe, with the recognition of the Czech Republic and Slovakia as independent states (formerly Czechoslovakia), and of Bosnia and Herzegovina, having now joined Croatia and Slovenia to have seceded from Yugoslavia. Many of what were hitherto republics of the USSR have become unitary states; and even as I write still more republics within the USSR are likely to join them. All the "new" countries formally recognized by the rest of the world community at the time of going to press are covered.

ED

AFGHANISTAN
The Islamic State of Afghanistan

The flag of this turbulent country has changed frequently during this century, primarily in terms of the detail of the emblem; common features from 1928 to 1992 have been the wheatears and rising sun, a central pulpit and niche from a mosque and scrollwork (sometimes with writing, sometimes without). In general, though, the overall pattern of three horizontal stripes was retained. A new flag was adopted in 1992 reflecting the religious foundation of the new regime, the inscription "God is Great" is on the green stripe, and "There is no God but Allah, and Mohammed is the Prophet Allah" is on the white stripe; the black is said to represent the country's dark past. All other emblems have been removed.

POPULATION: 15,513,000
CAPITAL: Kabul
AREA: 252,000 sq mi (652,000 km^2)
LANGUAGES: Pushtu, Dari (Persian)
RELIGION: Islam

ALBANIA
The Republic of Albania

The name "Shqipëria" (the Albanians' name for their country) means "land of the eagle"; the double-headed eagle features in the state coat of arms, having been adopted from the Byzantine emblem by Iskander Bey Skanderbeg (1403–68; known also as George Castriota), an Albanian patriot who drove the Turks from his native land around 1443 and kept them out until his death, whereupon his compatriots caved in and the country came once more under Turkish domination. The red background symbolizes the blood shed during this and other struggles for independence; the yellow outline star was added in 1946 when the country became a communist republic, but removed from the flag in 1992.

POPULATION: 3,150,000
CAPITAL: Tirana (Tiranë)
AREA: 11,100 sq mi (28,750 km^2)
LANGUAGE: Albanian
RELIGION: Islam minority; atheism official

ALGERIA
The Democratic and Popular Republic of Algeria

The present national flag of Algeria has been official since 1962; probably designed about 1928, it was from 1954 the flag of the independence fighters (the *Front de Libération Nationale*) and from 1958 that of the interim government. The background stripes are green, symbolizing Islam, and white, purity; these colours were also associated with Abd-el-Kader (1807–83), who, from 1832 until his surrender in 1847, led a bitter war of resistance against the French occupiers. Red commonly symbolizes bloodshed. The star and crescent are Islamic; the horns of the crescent are markedly longer than in most versions since, according to Algerian tradition, this lengthening implies good luck.

POPULATION: 23,850,000
CAPITAL: Algiers (Alger, El Djazair)
AREA: 920,000 sq mi (2,380,000 km^2)
LANGUAGES: Arabic; some French; some Berber
RELIGIONS: Islam; Christian minority

ANDORRA
The Principality of Andorra

Various possible explanations have been put forward for the colours of the three vertical stripes of the Andorran flag, but the most plausible would seem to be that they reflect the principality's joint Franco-Spanish suzerainty, blue and red reflecting the French flag and yellow and red reflecting the Spanish. The Andorran coat of arms, surmounted by a coronet, always appears superimposed on the central yellow stripe.

POPULATION: 51,000
CAPITAL: Andorra la Vella
AREA: 180 sq mi (465 km^2)
LANGUAGES: Catalan official language; French and Spanish widely used
RELIGION: Roman Catholic

ANGOLA
The Republic of Angola

The yellow motif in the centre of the flag is that of the Marxist MPLA (Popular Movement for the Liberation of Angola); comprising a machete, five-pointed star and the arc of a cogwheel, it is clearly inspired by the hammer and sickle used by the USSR (now Commonwealth of Independent States). Its yellowness is said to indicate the country's natural wealth. The juxtaposed red and black of the stripes are used in other communist-liberated nations to mean "Freedom or Death"; another explanation, peculiar to Angola, is that the black symbolizes Africa and the red the spilled blood of the freedom fighters.

POPULATION: 9,500,000
CAPITAL: Luanda (Loanda)
AREA: 482,500 sq mi (1,250,000 km^2)
LANGUAGES: Portuguese official language, Bantu
RELIGIONS: Christianity (mainly RC), Animism

ANTARCTICA

POPULATION: small, fluctuating and transitory
AREA: 5,445,000 sq mi (14,108,000 km^2)

New Zealand Territory
Ross Dependency

The New Zealand (*q.v.*) flag is flown.

French Southern & Antarctic Territory

The tricolour of France (*q.v.*) is flown.

Australian Antarctic Territory
Macquarie Islands and Heard and Macdonald Islands

The flag of Australia (*q.v.*) is used.

South African Territory
Prince Edward Island & Marion Island

The flag of the Republic of South Africa (*q.v.*) is flown.

Norwegian Dependency
(Queen Maud Land) Bouvet Island and Peter I Island

The flag of Norway (*q.v.*) is flown.

British Antarctic Territory

ANTIGUA AND BARBUDA

Introduced in 1967, when Antigua and Barbuda became an associated state (i.e., a self-governing dependency of the UK having the right to opt for independence) and unchanged on the gaining of independence in 1981, this flag is elaborately coded. The principal colour, red, represents the dynamism of the state's people. The inverted isosceles triangle forms a victory V, the victory being, of course, that over colonialism. Reading upwards, we have white sand, blue sea and the yellow-gold of the dawning sun of the new era. The blackness of the "sky" reflects the African heritage of the majority of the islands' people.

POPULATION: 82,500
CAPITAL: St John's
AREA: 170 sq mi (440 km^2)
LANGUAGE: English
RELIGION: Christianity (mainly Anglican)

ARGENTINA
The Argentine Republic

The emblem customarily appearing in the centre of the Argentinian flag is known as the Sun of May, and it represents the sun that shone through the clouds on 25 May 1810 when the people's first demonstrations against Spanish rule began; at or about the same time, the demonstrators adopted the colours blue and white. These colours were first formed into a triband flag in 1812 by General Manuel Belgrano (1770–1820), who for a couple of years was the leading light of the revolution, being succeeded in 1814 by José de San Martín (1778–1850). It was in 1818 that the Sun of May came to be superimposed on the white central stripe.

POPULATION: 32,000,000
CAPITAL: Buenos Aires
AREA: 1,080,000 sq mi (2,800,000 km^2)
LANGUAGE: Spanish
RELIGIONS: Christianity (mainly RC), Judaism

ARMENIA
The Republic of Armenia

Armenia has been a unitary state since 1991, having become so at the time of the general dissolution of the Union of Soviet Socialist Republics. Armenia was established in about the 8th century BC as an independent kingdom. In 328BC it was conquered by Alexander the Great and in 66BC by Rome; in AD303 it became the first country to adopt Christianity as its state religion, and the Armenian Church is still a distinct sect of Orthodox Christianity. Armenia's flag was first adopted in 1918 when the republic was previously independent. It had been abandoned when the republic became part of the USSR but was kept alive by use in exile. The design is supposed to recall the rainbow over Mount Ararat. The flag was re-adopted in 1990.

POPULATION: 3,283,000
CAPITAL: Yerevan
AREA: 11,600 sq mi (29,800 km^2)
LANGUAGES: Armenian, Russian, Turkish, Arabic
RELIGIONS: Christianity (Armenian Church), Judaism

AUSTRALIA
The Commonwealth of Australia

The five smaller stars in the Australian flag (created 1901 as the winning entry in a public competition; finally given royal assent 1954), which is based on the UK's Blue Ensign, represent the constellation of the Southern Cross. Four of the constellation's stars have seven points; the fifth has only five. The isolated seven-pointed star represents the Federal Commonwealth; until 1909 it had only six points, one for each of the states, but then the seventh was added to indicate the territories.

Australia has also the flag of the Australian Aborigines, devised in 1972. It shows a yellow disc (the sun) superimposed on two horizontal bands: the upper is black, for the Aborigines, and the lower is red, both for Aboriginal blood spilled and for the land itself.

POPULATION: 16,500,000
CAPITAL: Canberra
AREA: 2,970,000 sq mi (7,700,000 km^2)
LANGUAGES: English, Aboriginal
RELIGION: Christianity, Aboriginal

AUSTRALIA – STATES

New South Wales

Tasmania

Queensland

Victoria

South Australia

Western Australia

AUSTRALIA-ASSOCIATED LANDS

Australian Capital Territory

The Australian national flag is flown.

Coral Sea Islands Territory

The Australian national flag is flown.

Christmas Island

Norfolk Island

Cocos Islands

The Australian national flag is flown.

Northern Territory

AUSTRIA
The Republic of Austria

Legend has it that the red–white–red stripes of the Austrian flag, certainly one of the world's oldest, had their origin during the Third Crusade of 1189–92 when Duke Leopold V of Austria (1157–94), later to be the captor of Richard the Lionheart, fought so bloodily at the Battle of Acre (1191) that the only part of his costume to remain white was a band round his middle where his belt had been. The colours have been in use since at least 1230; they took their current form as the national flag in 1918, with the dissolution of the Austro-Hungarian Empire.

POPULATION: 7,600,000
CAPITAL: Vienna (Wien)
AREA: 32,360 sq mi (83,850 km²)
LANGUAGE: German
RELIGION: Christianity (mainly RC)

AZERBAIJAN
The Republic of Azerbaijan

Azerbaijan has been a unitary state since 1991, having become so at the time of the general dissolution of the Union of Soviet Socialist Republics. It is a land very rich in oil. The country's name, which means "Land of Flames", comes from the fact that in many areas natural gas seeps up directly from the ground. When Azerbaijan became independent once more in 1991, it used a flag very like that used during the previous period of independence (1918–20). The crescent and star proclaim the dominant religion, and the colours represent the aspirations of the nationalists. The eight points of the star represent the eight Turkish tribes of Azerbaijan.

POPULATION: 7,029,000
CAPITAL: Baku
AREA: 33,200 sq mi (86,000 km²)
LANGUAGE: Azeri
RELIGION: Islam

BAHAMAS
Commonwealth of the Bahamas

Introduced with the country's independence in 1973, the flag shows horizontal aquamarine stripes of sea above and a golden yellow band of sand/sun below. The intruding black triangle can be taken to represent either the resolve of the people to exploit their natural resources, or the people's unity and determination, or, most simply, the people themselves. Interestingly, a local pre-independence contest had failed to produce any design considered usable, and so this version was created using some of the ideas thrown up during the competition.

POPULATION: 245,000
CAPITAL: Nassau
AREA: 5400 sq mi (14,000 km²)
LANGUAGE: English
RELIGION: Christianity (various denominations)

BAHRAIN
The State of Bahrain

Before 1820 a number of the states around the Persian Gulf had the plain red flags of the Kharidjite sect of Islam. Many vessels flying such flags practised piracy on occidental ships, and so in that year the British decreed that in future all such vessels would be assumed to be pirates unless their flags bore white in addition to the red. The white on the Bahrain flag was initially a plain vertical stripe; the serration was introduced in 1932 for reasons that are unclear. It is also not clear why the Gulf pirates didn't simply add white to their flags and carry on plying their trade as before . . .

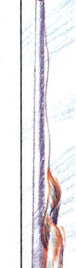

POPULATION: 430,000
CAPITAL: Al-Manamah (Manama)
AREA: 270 sq mi (690 km^2)
LANGUAGES: Arabic, English
RELIGIONS: Islam (minority Christian)

BANGLADESH
The People's Republic of Bangladesh

The basic design of this flag was introduced in 1971 when Bangladesh, until then East Pakistan, succeeded after a civil war in seceding from the rest of Pakistan. The 1971 version had, on the red disc, an outline map of the country in yellow; this was dropped in 1972. The disc itself, which is not quite centrally placed (it is slightly to the left of centre), is the sun of freedom and is red for the blood spilt in attaining that freedom. The green of the background has several explanations: it is an Islamic colour; it represents fertility; it symbolizes the youth of the country; it reflects the country's lushness.

The emblem of Bangladesh

POPULATION: 105,000,000
CAPITAL: Dacca (Dhaka)
AREA: 56,000 sq mi (144,000 km^2)
LANGUAGE: Bengali
RELIGIONS: Islam (majority), Hinduism, Buddhism, Christianity

BARBADOS

The central vertical stripe of golden yellow represents the sands of the country's beaches. The trident of Neptune, relating to the people's dependence on the bounty of the sea, dates back to colonial times, when it was used emblematically with a shaft; when the flag was introduced on independence (1966) the shaft was removed as a sign of the break with her past. The two blue stripes are for sea and sky.

POPULATION: 255,000
CAPITAL: Bridgetown
AREA: 165 sq mi (430 km^2)
LANGUAGE: English
RELIGION: Christianity (mainly Protestant)

BELARUS
The Republic of Belarus

Belarus has been a unitary state since 1991, having become so at the time of the general dissolution of the Union of Soviet Socialist Republics. By 1795 Byelorussia had become a part of the Russian Empire, and the eastern region of today's Belarus was made a part of the USSR in 1921, at which time the western region became a part of Poland; in 1945 this western region was annexed by the USSR. Before the dissolution of the USSR, Belarus was one of only two of the Soviet republics to have a separate vote at the UN. The colours of the new flag, first adopted in 1918 and kept alive in exile, are derived from the coat of arms.

POPULATION: 10,200,000
CAPITAL: Minsk
AREA: 81,150 sq mi (207,600 km²)
LANGUAGES: Polish, Russian
RELIGION: Christianity

BELGIUM
The Kingdom of Belgium

The Belgian flag is unusual in that it is almost square: the height and width are in the ratio 13:15. The black, yellow and red colours can be traced back to the arms of the provinces of Brabant, Flanders and Hainault. Arranged horizontally, they were used by the freedom fighters who succeeded in driving out the Austrians in 1789. Shortly afterwards, in 1792, the country was annexed by France, and in 1815 it was joined on to the Netherlands. In 1830 came independence and the vertical arrangement of the stripes, probably as an echo of the arrangement in the French tricolour. The shape and the arrangement were ratified in 1831.

POPULATION: 10,000,000
CAPITAL: Brussels (Bruxelles)
AREA: 11,800 sq mi (30,500 km²)
LANGUAGES: Flemish, French, German
RELIGION: Christianity (mainly RC)

BELIZE

This flag, adopted on independence in 1981, had as its precursor the flag of the People's United Party, which led the struggle for independence from 1950, a date reflected by the fifty laurel leaves surrounding the central arms. The thin red stripes at top and bottom of the flag were added to signify the minority opposition party, the United Democratic Party. The scroll beneath the shield bears the legend *Sub Umbra Floreo* ("I flourish in the shadows"). The two men supporting the shield are, on the right, a Creole bearing a paddle and on the left, a Mestizo bearing an axe. Behind them is a mahogany tree to stress the importance of timber in the state's economy, an element further underlined by the shield: top left, a paddle and hammer; top right, a saw and felling axe; bottom, a sailing ship taking timber to Europe.

POPULATION: 176,000
CAPITAL: Belmopan
AREA: 8,900 sq mi (23,000 km²)
LANGUAGES: English, Creole, Spanish, Mayan
RELIGION: Christianity

BENIN
The Republic of Benin

The design of the Benin flag was adopted in 1975, three years after Lt-Col Mathieu Kerékou (1933–) had swept to power in the last of a long succession of military coups since Dahomey (as it then was) had gained independence within the French community in 1960. He established Marxism-Leninism as the system of government in 1974, and in 1975 the country's new name and new flag appeared. The overall green reflects the fact that the nation is predominantly agricultural and together the green, red and yellow are the Pan African colours.

POPULATION: 4,450,000
CAPITAL: Porto Novo
AREA: 44,000 sq mi (112,500 km^2)
LANGUAGES: French, a spectrum of African languages
RELIGIONS: Animism, Christianity, Islam.

BHUTAN
The Kingdom of Bhutan

The wingless dragon of the flag is Bhutan's national symbol; the literal meaning of the kingdom's Tibetan name, Druk-yul, is "Land of the Dragon". Although the colours of the two triangles have varied, the current saffron yellow is an expression of the king's authority and the orange-red the spiritual power of Buddhism, the country's predominant religion.

POPULATION: 1,450,000
CAPITAL: Thimphu (Thimbu)
AREA: 18,000 sq mi (46,600 km^2)
LANGUAGES: Nepali, English, Dzongkha
RELIGIONS: Buddhism, Hinduism, Islam

BOLIVIA
The Republic of Bolivia

Bolivia was called Upper Peru until 1825, when it gained independence from the Spaniards, and Simón Bolívar (1783–1830), for whom the country was given its new name, became first president of the free nation; very soon afterwards the Bolivians realized that the exchange had not been altogether advantageous, and Bolívar in turn was driven out. The 1825 colours were, from the top, red, green and red, the green dominating the area; the following year the upper red stripe became yellow, and in 1851 the stripes became of equal area and adopted the current red, yellow, green arrangement. The red signifies the courage of the liberating army, the yellow the country's resources of metals, and the green the country's agricultural richness.

POPULATION: 7,000,000
CAPITAL: La Paz
AREA: 425,000 sq mi (1,100,000 km^2)
LANGUAGES: Spanish, Quechua, Aymara
RELIGION: Christianity (mainly RC)

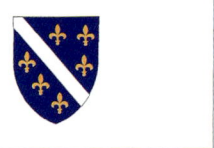

BOSNIA AND HERZEGOVINA
The Republic of Bosnia and Herzegovina

POPULATION: 4,366,000
CAPITAL: Sarajevo
AREA: 19,750 sq mi (51,129 km²)
LANGUAGES: Serbo-Croat
RELIGIONS: Moslem, Greek Orthodox, Catholic

Bosnia and Herzegovina is a land-locked country lying between Croatia and Serbia and currently being fought over by both of these ex-Yugoslav states. It had been part of the Ottoman Empire from 1463 to 1876, when it was occupied by Austria. It was united with Yugoslavia in 1918 and became a socialist republic in 1946. Following the general dissolution of Yugoslavia, Bosnia and Herzegovina declared its independence in 1992. Its flag depicts the arms of King Stephen Tvrtko, who ruled Bosnia and Herzegovina at the time of the struggle with the Turks. His family were related to the Anjou dynasty which ruled at that time in Hungary, hence the fleur-de-lys.

BOTSWANA
The Republic of Botswana

POPULATION: 1,100,000
CAPITAL: Gaborone
AREA: 231,700 sq mi (600,300 km²)
LANGUAGES: English, Setswana
RELIGIONS: indigenous religions (Christian minority)

Botswana's flag was adopted on independence in 1966, and the central band of black with white on either side indicates the racial harmony to which the new nation aspired; its first president, Sir Seretse Khama (1921–80), had married an Englishwoman, so the aspiration was not just an empty ideal, despite the far from harmonious relations between the races in surrounding nations, notably South Africa, on which the country's economy is heavily reliant. The overall blue expresses the concepts of sky and water, fused to represent rain: Botswana is a very arid country, and consequently the life-giving rain is of vital importance to its people – even the national motto, "Let there be rain", stresses this.

BRAZIL
The Federative Republic of Brazil

POPULATION: 144,500,000
CAPITAL: Brasilia
AREA: 3,280,000 sq mi (8,500,000 km²)
LANGUAGE: Portuguese
RELIGIONS: Christianity (mainly RC), Voodoo

For a long time the Portuguese owned Brazil; when they went home in 1821 they left behind them King John VI's second son, Pedro, as prince-regent. A year later he declared Brazil's independence and was crowned its first emperor. Pedro I's first flag for Brazil was of green with a yellow lozenge, as in the modern version, but with the royal arms in the centre of the lozenge. The current design in the lozenge was adopted when the country became a Republic, the stars representing the states. The motto, *Ordem e Progresso*, means "Order and Progress".

BRUNEI
Brunei Darussalam

The flag of the Sultan of Brunei was originally a plain yellow. The country came under British protection in 1888, and in 1906 the diagonal black-and-white stripe was superimposed to denote that the sultan did not have absolute power, but shared it with two viziers. The coat of arms of Brunei was added in 1959, when Brunei became self-governing. It is a complex design showing a winged pillar surmounted by a pair of wings that are themselves surmounted by a flagged umbrella; the pillar is framed by a crescent bearing the state motto, "Always serve with the guidance of God"; beneath the crescent is a scroll bearing the legend "Brunei – home of peace", and to either side of it are half-spread hands to indicate the goodwill of the government.

POPULATION: 241,500
CAPITAL: Bandar Seri Begawan
AREA: 2230 sq mi (5770 km^2)
LANGUAGES: Malay, Chinese, English
RELIGIONS: Islam, Buddhism, Christianity

BULGARIA
The Republic of Bulgaria

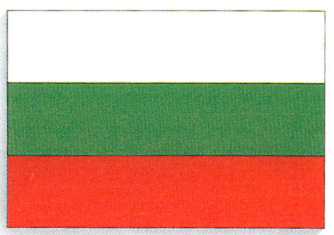

The three-banded arrangement for this flag was adopted in 1878 when Slavic armies helped drive the Turkish occupiers out of Bulgaria; the colours are white for peace, green for freedom and red for the blood of those who attained that freedom. The national emblem was added in 1947, and has undergone modifications since. The rampant lion has been Bulgaria's symbol since the 14th century; the wheatears and the arc of a cogwheel represent, respectively, agriculture and industrialization, and the union between the workers in both spheres. In 1990, with the end of the Communist regime, the old emblem was removed, leaving a plain tricolour.

POPULATION: 9,000,000
CAPITAL: Sofia
AREA: 42,800 sq mi (111,000 km^2)
LANGUAGES: Bulgarian, Turkish
RELIGIONS: Christianity, Islam (both minorities)

BURKINA FASO
The People's Democratic Republic of Burkina Faso

The red, green and yellow of this flag are the Pan-African colours, and they signify fellowship with other ex-colonial African nations. This flag was adopted in 1984, after the coup of 1983, which brought the mixed civilian-military government of Captain Thomas Sankara to power; along with the new flag came the new name of the country (which had previously been Upper Volta): Burkina Faso means "The Land of The Honest People" or "The Republic of Upright Men". Unfortunately some of the "upright men", to the dismay of the majority, in 1987 overthrew Sankara – a popular, active and reforming socialist leader – in a coup led by Captain Blaise Compaoré. The five-pointed star can be taken to symbolize either freedom or revolution.

POPULATION: 9,000,000
CAPITAL: Ouagadougou
AREA: 105,000 sq mi (275,000 km^2)
LANGUAGES: French, various African languages
RELIGIONS: indigenous religions, Islam, Christianity

BURMA
The Union of Myanmar

Since 1991 Burma has been known as Myanmar by its people. In 1948 it gained its independence from the UK, setting up as a democratic republic. In 1962 a military coup overthrew democracy, and in 1974 a one-party socialist republic was set up. Since 1988 the country's president has been General Saw Maung, despite the fact that Daw Aung San Suu Kyi (1945–), herself under house arrest since 1989, won a landslide victory in elections held in 1990. The present design of the flag dates from the new constitution of 1974, differing from the 1948 flag only in regard to the emblem on the blue rectangle. This now shows a rice plant set in front of a 14-toothed cogwheel (the seven states and seven provinces), which is surrounded by a ring of stars, one per tooth.

POPULATION: 40,000,000
CAPITAL: Rangoon (Yangon)
AREA: 261,000 sq mi (676,500 km²)
LANGUAGE: Burmese
RELIGION: Buddhism

BURUNDI
The Republic of Burundi

The colours of the Burundi flag, which reached its modern form in 1967, are white for peace, green for hope and red for the independence struggle and the sacrifices made by the people prior to the gaining of that independence in 1962. The three green-rimmed red stars stand for the three words of the national motto – "Unity, Work, Progress" – and also for the three peoples of Burundi, the Tutsi, the Hutu and the Twa. The reality of the state has belied these pacific ideals: the pygmy Twa, the country's aborigines, have virtually disappeared, and the Tutsi and the Hutu have disputed power bloodily ever since independence.

POPULATION: 5,200,000
CAPITAL: Bujumbura
AREA: 10,750 sq mi (28,000 km²)
LANGUAGES: Kirundi, French, Swahili, Bantu
RELIGIONS: Christianity (mostly RC), indigenous religions (Islam minority)

CAMBODIA

Before 1989 the flag of Cambodia featured a plain red background with a silhouette of the famous Angkor Wat – the main temple, dating from the 12th century, of the ruined city of Angkor, founded in the late 9th century as capital of the Khmer Empire – with two steps on each side of five towers. The number of towers distinguished this flag, adopted in 1978 by the Vietnam-controlled puppet government of the National United Front for the Salvation of Kampuchea (as Cambodia was then known), from the very similar three-towered version flown in 1975–8 when the country was suffering under the regime of Pol Pot (1926–) and his Khmer Rouge. In 1989, with the withdrawal of the Vietnamese, the current "flag of national unity" was introduced, retaining Angkor Wat's five towers but now on a background of red and blue.

POPULATION: 7,900,000
CAPITAL: Phnom Penh
AREA: 70,000 sq mi (181,000 km²)
LANGUAGES: Khmer, French
RELIGIONS: Buddhism, Islam

CAMEROON
The Republic of Cameroon

The green, red and yellow of the Cameroon flag are the Pan-African colours. The flag's form is based on the French tricolour, reflecting the fact that before 1960 the country was divided in two, the larger French Cameroon and the smaller British Cameroon. In that year the French part became the independent Cameroon Republic; in 1961 part of the British section federated with the young republic (the other part of it opted to join Nigeria), and two small yellow stars were added to the flag's central stripe. In 1975 the two parts became fully united, and the two stars became a single, larger one.

POPULATION: 10,800,000
CAPITAL: Yaoundé
AREA: 183,500 sq mi (475,400 km²)
LANGUAGES: French, English, local languages
RELIGIONS: Christianity, indigenous religions, Islam

CANADA

The present maple leaf flag was adopted in 1965. Before that Canada made use of the British Red Ensign with the Canadian arms. The prime minister, Lester Pearson, believed that this was not sufficiently distinctive, or representative of Canada as a multi-ethnic nation and a long and complex political struggle ensued to design a new flag that would be accepted, in the face of opposition from those who wanted to keep the Red Ensign. The design attained its purpose: to be of a uniquely Canadian character, showing no affinities to either France or the UK. Curiously, the red verticals on either side of the maple leaf (the long-time national symbol) represent the Atlantic and Pacific oceans; they were originally intended to be blue, but altered so that the flag would accord with what had been the official colours of Canada since 1921.

POPULATION: 26,000,000
CAPITAL: Ottawa
AREA: 3,850,350 sq mi (9,975,000 km²)
LANGUAGES: English, French
RELIGIONS: Christianity

CANADA
Provinces and Territories

Alberta

British Columbia

Manitoba

New Brunswick

CANADA
Provinces and Territories

Newfoundland

Prince Edward Island

Northwest Territories

Quebec

Novia Scotia

Saskatchewan

Ontario

Yukon Territory

CAPE VERDE
The Republic of Cape Verde

A new flag was adopted in 1992, when Cape Verde finally severed links with Guinea-Bissau. The new flag has 10 stars representing the islands, set in a blue sea. Prior to 1992, the similarity between the two nations' flags was explained by the fact that both were derived from the flag of the Partido Africano da Independencia da Guiné e Cabo Verde (PAIGC), the liberation movement which succeeded in gaining independence for both countries (Guinea-Bissau in 1974, Cape Verde in 1975). PAIGC's aim had been that the two nations should unite, but this merger was scotched in 1980 by a military coup in Guinea-Bissau.

POPULATION: 360,000
CAPITAL: Praia
AREA: 1560 sq mi (4030 km^2)
LANGUAGES: Portuguese, Crioulo
RELIGIONS: Christianity (mainly RC)

CENTRAL AFRICAN REPUBLIC

The Pan-African colours are red, yellow and green; those of the French tricolour are red, white and blue. The flag of the Central African Republic (formerly part of French Equatorial Africa) brings together both colour schemes in a single flag, with the shared red vertical stripe. The intention was to encourage a partnership between, on the one hand, a union of the Central African Republic and the other states that had once been part of French Equatorial Africa and, on the other, France herself. Such an African union – expressed by the yellow star at top left – has, of course, not come about. The flag was adopted in 1958, two years before independence.

POPULATION: 2,770,000
CAPITAL: Bangui
AREA: 240,000 sq mi (623,000 km^2)
LANGUAGES: French, Sango
RELIGIONS: indigenous religions, Christianity (Islam minority)

CHAD
The Republic of Chad

Adopted in 1959, the year before independence, the flag of Chad is much like the French tricolour but with a compromise in terms of the colours used: red and blue from the French scheme and red and yellow from the Pan-African colours. The red can be taken to represent the sacrifice for freedom, yellow both the desert of the nation's north and the bright sun, and blue the clear, tropical sky.

POPULATION: 5,400,000
CAPITAL: Ndjamena (N'Djamena)
AREA: 495,700 sq mi (1,284,000 km^2)
LANGUAGES: French, Arabic, indigenous languages
RELIGIONS: Islam, indigenous religions (Christian minority)

CHILE
The Republic of Chile

The Chilean flag is based on that used by the country's independence movement, which eventually succeeded on 1 January 1818. The real inspiration for both the earlier flag and the version adopted in 1818, however, seems almost certainly to have been the Stars and Stripes (which bore fewer stars in those days!) – indeed, according to one version of the flag's history the creative genius behind it was that of a US national, Charles Wood, who was serving among the freedom fighters. The almost-finalized flag, without the star, was in use for a few months before being officially adopted on independence day, when the star was added. The colours are supposed to represent the blood shed by the rebels, the snow of the Andean peaks and the sky.

POPULATION: 12,750,000
CAPITAL: Santiago
AREA: 292,270 sq mi (757,000 km^2)
LANGUAGE: Spanish
RELIGION: Christianity (mainly RC)

CHINA
The People's Republic of China

This flag was introduced in 1949 on the declaration of the People's Republic of China by the triumphant communists. Red and yellow are traditional colours of China and, of course, red is also the colour of communism. The large five-pointed star represents the Communist Party's programme, while the four smaller ones are for the four sections of society that, it was claimed, would be united by and would unite to carry through that programme; the four classes were the peasantry, the workers, the bourgeoisie and those capitalists who would participate in the on-going revolution. The similarity in the flag's basic design with that of the now defunct Union of Soviet Socialist Republic's is, naturally, no coincidence.

POPULATION: 1,105,000,000
CAPITAL: Beijing
AREA: 3,706,000 sq mi (9,600,000 km²)
LANGUAGES: Chinese languages, Tibetan, Mongolian, Uygur, Miao, Zhuang, Yao
RELIGIONS: Atheism; Confucianism; Buddhism, Taoism, Islam, Christianity

COLOMBIA
The Republic of Colombia

The similarities between the flag of Colombia and those of Ecuador and Venezuela (*qq.v.*) are not coincidental. These countries, along with Panama, were once the vast Spanish territory of New Granada. Simón Bolívar (1783–1830), the Liberator, secured the independence of the territory in 1819–21, and it was named Greater Colombia. The yellow, blue and red colours were those adopted by the Venezuelan freedom fighter Francisco de Miranda (1750–1816) to convey the message that the nation (yellow) was separated by the sea (blue) from Spain, the red seemingly indicating both the liberation of the South American territories and the blood of their people. The current version of the Colombian flag was introduced in 1861.

POPULATION: 30,250,000
CAPITAL: Bogotá
AREA: 439,800 sq mi (1,139,000 km²)
LANGUAGE: Spanish
RELIGION: Christianity (mainly RC)

COMOROS
The Federal and Islamic Republic of the Comoros

Adopted in 1978, the flag of the Comoros uses the Islamic colour green and the Islamic symbol of the crescent. The four stars symbolize the four main islands of the group, which attained independence in 1975; one of those four islands, Mayotte, in fact chose to remain a French dependency, but the number of stars was not amended – presumably in the hope that Mayotte may one day change its mind.

POPULATION: 487,000
CAPITAL: Moroni (Njazidja)
AREA: 838 sq mi (2170 km²)
LANGUAGES: Swahili, Arabic, French
RELIGION: Islam

CONGO
The Republic of Congo

In 1991 Congo reverted to the original flag it used in 1960, when the state became independent. This is in the Pan-African colours but in a distinct arrangement. From 1970 to 1991 a different flag was in use: red with a crossed hammer and hoe, and a gold star with a wreath, this symbolised the communist regime then in power, which has now been replaced by a multiparty democracy.

POPULATION: 1,890,000
CAPITAL: Brazzaville
AREA: 132,000 sq mi (342,000 km^2)
LANGUAGES: French, local languages
RELIGIONS: Christianity, indigenous religions

COSTA RICA
The Republic of Costa Rica

Until 1821 Costa Rica was part of the captaincy-general of Guatemala ruled by Spain; when the captaincy-general declared independence but was almost immediately swallowed up by the Mexican Empire. By 1824 Costa Rica, El Salvador, Guatemala, Honduras and Nicaragua – had regained their freedom and formed the Central American Federation that was soon to be unravelled, in 1838. Costa Rica has adopted the blue and white of the CAF flag, although in a different arrangement. In 1848 the flag included a central red stripe in honour of the ousting of Louis Philippe (1773–1850) as King of the French. The arms depict the rising sun of freedom, three volcanoes, seven stars (for seven provinces) and two sailing ships.

POPULATION: 2,850,000
CAPITAL: San José
AREA: 19,600 sq mi (51,000 km^2)
LANGUAGE: Spanish
RELIGION: Christianity (almost exclusively RC)

CROATIA
The Republic of Croatia

Croatia seceded from Yugoslavia (*q.v.*) in 1991 at the end of a period of civil war that was short but on occasion extremely brutal. As a monarchy, Croatia had a long period of stability from 1102 until 1849, being an autonomous kingdom under the Hungarian crown; it was then successively an Austrian crownland and (1868) a Hungarian crownland before the formation of Yugoslavia. Croatia's flag shares the red, white and blue used in most Slav countries. It is distinguished by the arms in the centre, which comprise a large shield of Croatia surmounted by five smaller shields representing (from left to right) Croatia Ancient, Dubrovnik, Dalmatia, Istria and Slavonia. The flag was adopted in 1990 for the new state which became independent in 1991.

POPULATION: 4,601,469
CAPITAL: Zagreb
AREA: 21,820 sq mi (56,550 km^2)
LANGUAGE: Serbo-Croat
RELIGION: Christianity (almostly exclusively Roman Catholic)

CUBA
The Republic of Cuba

The ironic similarity between the "Lone Star" flag of Cuba and the Stars and Stripes of its arch enemy, the USA, is far from coincidental. The design can be traced to 1849 and General Narciso López (d1851), a Venezuelan filibuster who, living in the USA, was anxious to liberate Cuba from the Spanish and claim it for his adopted country – hence the single star, to be added to the others. The red triangle symbolized freedom from the Spanish and the blood that would have to be shed to attain it; the three sides represent liberty, fraternity and equality. The Spanish left the island in 1898, at which time López's design was adopted, and for three years Cuba was occupied by the USA before gaining full independence in 1901 (declared 1902).

POPULATION: 10,400,000
CAPITAL: Havana
AREA: 44,200 sq mi (114,500 km^2)
LANGUAGE: Spanish
RELIGION: Christianity (mainly RC)

CYPRUS
The Republic of Cyprus

The flag of Cyprus, adopted on independence in 1960, expresses a hope rather than a reality. The declaration of independence and the adoption of the flag came after a period of terrorism waged by the Greek Cypriots against the British, in order to regain union with Greece. The large Turkish minority made such an end unthinkable, so independence was granted as a compromise. The olive branches and the white background had clear meanings of peace and harmony between the two communities, an ideal that has never been attained. The two parts have used the Greek and Turkish national flags, although the official flag shown here is used abroad. The copper colouring of the central map reflects the meaning of the island's name, "Copper Isle".

POPULATION: 700,000
CAPITAL: Nicosia
AREA: 3570 sq mi (9250 km^2)
LANGUAGES: Greek, Turkish, English
RELIGIONS: Christianity (mainly Greek Orthodox), Islam

CZECH REPUBLIC

The Czech Republic became a unitary state in January 1993; formerly part of Czechoslovakia which has now divided into two: The Czech Republic and Slovakia. Czechoslovakia was formed in 1918, after the collapse of the Austrio-Hungarian Empire out of the Austrian possessions Bohemia, Moravia and part of Silesia, and Hungarian possessions Slovakia and Ruthenia. World War II effected further changes, including the loss of Ruthenia to the USSR; in 1948 communism triumphed, and in 1969 the nation's two separate republics, Slovakia and The Czech Socialist Republic were established. The 1918 flag of Czechoslovakia was that of Bohemia-Moravia, in red and white, and the first official flag (1920) incorporated a blue triangle to represent the Slav population. This flag has been retained as the official flag.

POPULATION: 10,311,000
CAPITAL: Prague (Praha)
AREA: 30,500 sq mi (78,864 km^2)
LANGUAGES: Czech, Hungarian, Slovak
RELIGIONS: Christian (Roman Catholic and Protestant)

DENMARK
The Kingdom of Denmark

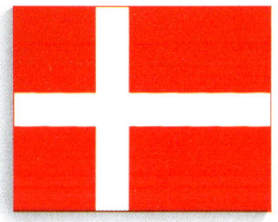

Although there is a traditional legend about the Danish flag having fallen from heaven during a battle between the Danes and the Baltic pagans in the 13th century, it is in fact a crusader's flag. First used in the arms of King Valdemar IV Atterdag (1340–1375) it became known as the *Dannebrog* literally meaning "Danish cloth". It was originally square in form, but the design became elongated, and the arm of the cross at the flying end was extended. The flags of the other Scandinavian countries are derived directly or indirectly from this model, so that this distinctive form of cross has become known as the Scandinavian cross.

POPULATION: 5,130,000
CAPITAL: Copenhagen (København)
AREA: 16,600 sq mi (43,000 km^2)
LANGUAGE: Danish
RELIGION: Christianity (almost exclusively Evangelical Lutheran)

DENMARK ASSOCIATED LANDS

Faeroe Islands
Føroyar

Greenland
Grønland

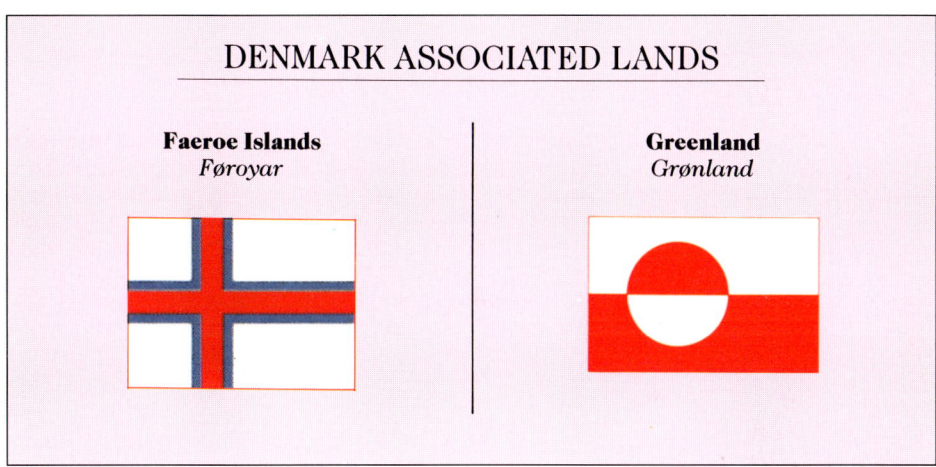

DJIBOUTI
The Republic of Djibouti

The two ethnic groups of Djibouti are the majority Issas and the minority Afars – before gaining independence in 1977 the country was for a time known as the French Territory of the Afars and the Issas. The two groups came together in 1972 as the Popular African League for Independence (LPAI), dedicated to fighting for freedom, and adopted the current national flag, which has the traditional blue of the Issas and the traditional green of the Afars, along with white for peace and the red five-pointed star for unity.

POPULATION: 456,000
CAPITAL: Djibouti
AREA: 8880 sq mi (23,000 km^2)
LANGUAGES: Arabic, French, Somali, Afar
RELIGION: Islam

DOMINICA
The Commonwealth of Dominica

The device at the centre of Dominica's flag is adapted from the coat of arms, adopted in 1961 and, before the country's independence in 1978, used on the British Blue Ensign to form the national flag. The parrot is a sisserou, the national bird, a species – *Amazona imperialis* – not known outside the island. The redness of the disc is for socialism, and the ten stars surrounding the sisserou are for the island's 10 parishes. The green background represents the country's lush vegetation. The cross is of Christian origin, its tripleness symbolizing the Holy Trinity; its colours are black for the African origins of most of the population, yellow for the Carib aboriginals and white for peace and purity.

POPULATION: 94,000
CAPITAL: Roseau
AREA: 290 sq mi (750 km²)
LANGUAGES: English, French
RELIGION: Christianity (mainly RC)

DOMINICAN REPUBLIC

Between 1822 and 1844 what is now the Dominican Republic was under the rule of conquering Haiti (*q.v.*), whose flag then had two horizontal bands, blue above and red beneath. In 1839 the liberation movement La Trinitaria amended the Haitian flag for its own use by superimposing a white cross (for sacrifice, faith, etc.) as well as 10 white stars, which vanished when independence was declared in 1844. The superimposition of the cross formed a pair of blue rectangles above a pair of red rectangles; this arrangement was later altered to the current one.

POPULATION: 6,750,000
CAPITAL: Santo Domingo
AREA: 18,700 sq mi (48,430 km²)
LANGUAGE: Spanish
RELIGION: Christianity (almost exclusively RC)

ECUADOR
The Republic of Ecuador

The story of the flag of Ecuador is much the same as that of the flag of Colombia (*q.v.*, and see also Venezuela). The yellow, blue and red colours were those adopted by the Venezuelan freedom fighter Francisco de Miranda (1750–1816) – he fought in the American Revolutionary War and the French Revolution as well as the Spanish-American Revolution – to convey the message that the nation (yellow) was separated by the sea (blue) from Spain, the red indicating both the liberation of the South American territories and the blood their people were willing to shed in attaining that freedom. The current version of the Ecuadorian flag, which is identical with the Colombian except for its narrower shape was adopted in 1900.

POPULATION: 10,200,000
CAPITAL: Quito
AREA (excluding the Galapagos Islands): 110,000 sq mi (284,000 km²)
LANGUAGES: Spanish, indigenous languages
RELIGION: Christianity (mainly RC)

EGYPT
The Arab Republic of Egypt

The flag is in the Pan-Arab colours but without the green; the original flag of Egypt was itself green, and in the early years of the use of the tricolour (1952–8) the two were always flown together. In 1958, however, Egypt and Syria formed the United Arab Republic, with North Yemen. Syria and North Yemen withdrew almost immediately, in 1961, but Egypt continued to use the name and the flag until 1971, when she, Syria and Libya formed the Federation of Arab Republics. Egypt retained the Federation flag even after 1977, when the other two countries left in disgust at Egypt's growing desire to make peace with Israel (which she effected in 1979). In 1984 the golden Eagle of Saladin, from Egypt's own arms, replaced the hawk.

POPULATION: 52,000,000
CAPITAL: Cairo (El Qâhira)
AREA: 386,700 sq mi (1,001,500 km²)
LANGUAGES: Arabic, Berber, Nubian, Beja
RELIGION: Islam (Christian minority)

EL SALVADOR
The Republic of El Salvador

Until 1821 El Salvador was part of the captaincy-general of Guatemala, ruled by Spain; in that year the captaincy-general declared independence but was almost immediately swallowed up by the Mexican Empire. By 1824 El Salvador – with Costa Rica, Guatemala, Honduras and Nicaragua – had regained their freedom and formed the Central American Federation, an arrangement that was soon to be unravelled, in 1838. The flag of the CAF was a simple blue and white triband, and it was to this design that El Salvador turned in 1912. The flag may be used plain, with the motto "God, Union, Liberty" or with the national arms, which show flags and, in a triangular frame, volcanoes, a rainbow (peace) and the Cap of Liberty.

POPULATION: 5,200,000
CAPITAL: San Salvador
AREA: 8100 sq mi (21,000 km²)
LANGUAGES: Spanish, indigenous languages
RELIGION: Christianity (almost exclusively RC)

EQUATORIAL GUINEA
The Republic of Equatorial Guinea

Equatorial Guinea was one of the last colonial territories in Africa to gain independence, which it did in 1968 from the Spanish; it adopted its current flag at the same time. As one might expect, the green stands for agriculture, the white for peace, the red for liberation and the blue for the sea. The central emblem – altered during 1978–9, but then reinstated after a military coup that ousted (and executed) President Francisco Macias Nguema (1924–79) – is the state arms, comprising a kapok (or "God") tree with six stars above it to represent the five islands and the mainland territory that make up the nation and, below, a scroll bearing the motto *Unidad Paz Justicia* ("Unity, Peace, Justice").

POPULATION: 420,000
CAPITAL: Malabo
AREA: 10,800 sq mi (28,000 km²)
LANGUAGES: Spanish, indigenous languages
RELIGIONS: Christianity (mainly RC), indigenous religions

ESTONIA
The Republic of Estonia

Estonia has been a unitary state since 1991, having become so at the time of the general dissolution of the Union of Soviet Socialist Republics. During its earlier history it was ruled at various times by the Danes, the Teutonic Knights, the Swedes and the Russians. The flag of Estonia dates back to 1881 and became widely used as a national symbol until in 1918 when independence was secured. Subsequently Estonia was occupied in turn by the Germans and the Soviet Union from 1940 onwards, becoming a Soviet Socialist Republic. The old national flag was restored in 1988 and officially adopted in 1990.

POPULATION: 1,573,000
CAPITAL: Tallinn
AREA: 17,400 sq mi (45,100 km²)
LANGUAGES: Estonian, Russian
RELIGION: Christianity

ETHIOPIA
The People's Democratic Republic of Ethiopia

The country has a very long history, but the story of modern Ethiopia really begins in 1941 when Haile Selassie I (1892–1977), who had earlier ruled 1930–36, was restored to the throne. His role in modernizing the country cannot be overstated, and his importance in encouraging the Pan-African cause is manifest, but was deposed by a military coup in 1974. Since then the country has been tormented by civil war and famine. Before his coronation the emperor was Prince Ras Tafari, regarded by many as divine, and Ethiopia as a promised land. The Ethiopian flag, adopted in 1897 but with the colours in the reverse order, was responsible for the introduction of the Pan-African colours.

POPULATION: 48,000,000
CAPITAL: Addis Ababa
AREA: 472,000 sq mi (1,222,000 km²)
LANGUAGES: Amharic, Galla, Arabic, Sidamo
RELIGIONS: Islam, Christianity (Coptic), indigenous religions

FIJI
The Republic of Fiji

The islands were discovered in 1643 by the Dutch explorer Abel Tasman (1603–59). In the late 19th century the trade in sandalwood brought many visitors to the islands, and greed-inspired rioting became rife; Fiji ceded to the UK in 1874 to bring this under control, and it was almost a century later that the state regained its independence. The flag, adopted in 1970, managed to survive the cession of Fiji to the UK, the regaining of independence and, in 1987, the departure of the nation from the Commonwealth. The design is clearly based on the British Blue Ensign, although the background shade is much paler than is customary. Also incorporated is the shield of the arms.

POPULATION: 727,000
CAPITAL: Suva
AREA: 7100 sq mi (18,400 km²)
LANGUAGES: English, Fijian, Hindustani, Tamil, Urdu, Chinese
RELIGIONS: Christianity, Hinduism, Islam

FINLAND
The Republic of Finland

Finland has a version of the Scandinavian Cross, seen also in the flags of Iceland, Norway, Sweden and Denmark (*q.v.*). The Finnish version – in blue and white for lakes and snowscapes – was first adopted in 1863, the same year that Finnish was recognized as the official language of the troubled country, then a part of Russia. Independence and internal strife came in 1917, and so it was not until 1919 and the establishment of the republic that the flag was once more officially adopted.

POPULATION: 4,960,000
CAPITAL: Helsinki (Helsingfors)
AREA: 130,100 sq mi (337,000 km^2)
LANGUAGES: Finnish, Swedish
RELIGION: Christianity (mainly Lutheran)

FRANCE
The French Republic

With the Stars and Stripes, the Red Flag and the Union Jack, the French tricolor is one of the best known of all the flags of the world. The present flag dates from 1794 – the design was by Jacques-Louis David (1748–1825) at the behest of the Convention – but originated a few years earlier, in 1789, when Louis XVI (1754–93) brought the colours together by adding the blue and red of Paris to the white of the Bourbons. The flag has not been in constant use since 1794; there have been lacunae in 1814–15 and in 1815– 30, and the relative widths of the stripes were varied from 1853 until legally enshrined as equal in 1946. The simple arrangement and/or the colours have inspired the flags of nations the world over.

POPULATION: 55,900,000
CAPITAL: Paris
AREA: 212,900 sq mi (551,500 km^2)
LANGUAGE: French (minority tongues include Basque, Breton, Catalan, Corsican)
RELIGION: Christianity (mainly RC)

FRANCE – ASSOCIATED LANDS

French Guiana
The French tricolour is used.

French Polynesia

Guadeloupe and Dependencies
The French tricolour is used.

Martinique
The French tricolour, together with a local flag, is used.

New Caledonia
The French tricolour is used.

Reunion
The French tricolour is used.

Saint Pierre et Miquelon
The French tricolour, together with a local flag, is used.

Wallis and Futuna Islands
The French tricolour, together with a local flag, is used.

GABON
The Gabonese Republic

Gabon became an autonomous republic within the French Community in 1958 and gained full independence in 1960. The immediate predecessor of the modern flag was chosen in the brief interim period between the two statuses, and had the same colour scheme, although with a narrower yellow band and with the French tricolour superimposed on the green band. Today's version was adopted on independence. The green is for forestry and the blue for the Atlantic; the yellow is for both the sun and the Equator, which passes through Gabon.

POPULATION: 1,200,000
CAPITAL: Libreville
AREA: 103,000 sq mi (266,000 km^2)
LANGUAGES: French, Bantu
RELIGIONS: Christianity, indigenous religions

THE GAMBIA
The Republic of The Gambia

The Gambian flag, adopted when the country gained its independence from the UK in 1965, is roughly similar in construction to that of Botswana (*q.v.*). The colours are intended to represent the Gambia River (blue) as it flows through lushly vegetated land (green), with the sun beating down overhead (red). By intention, these colours have no political connotations whatsoever.

POPULATION: 815,000
CAPITAL: Banjul
AREA: 4,360 sq mi (11,300 km^2)
LANGUAGES: English, indigenous languages
RELIGION: Islam

GEORGIA
The Republic of Georgia

Georgia has been a unitary state since 1991, having become so at the time of the general dissolution of the Union of Soviet Socialist Republics. When under Roman rule it was invaded by the Persians; then came the Arabs until independence was achieved in the 10th century, although thereafter there were invasions by the Tartars, Persians and Turks until 1801, when Georgia was annexed by Russia. An independent kingdom from 1801 Georgia's flag of cherry red, white and black dates from 1918 when it freed itself from Russia. This lasted until 1921 when the Soviet Union regained Georgia. The flag was restored in 1990 and became that of the newly independent state in 1991.

POPULATION: 6,379,000
CAPITAL: Tbilisi
AREA: 27,700 sq mi (69,700 km^2)
LANGUAGES: Georgian, Russian
RELIGION: Orthodox Christianity

GERMANY
The Federal Republic of Germany

On reunification in 1990 to form the new Federal Republic of Germany, the former West Germany and East Germany (German Democratic Republic) opted to retain not only the West's national name but also its flag. In fact, this flag had been used by united Germany for various periods much earlier, notably during the Weimar Republic (1919–33); it was reintroduced by both Germanies in 1949, the flag of the East differing only in that, from 1959, a communist emblem was added. When the flag was used during 1848 – the "year of revolutions" in Germany's history – the colours were described by politician and poet Ferdinand Freiligrath (1810–76) as: black for gunpowder, red for blood and "the flame has a golden glow".

POPULATION: 76,000,000
CAPITAL: Berlin
AREA: 138,000 sq mi (358,000 km^2)
LANGUAGE: German
RELIGION: Christianity (Islamic minority)

GHANA
The Republic of Ghana

Ghana was the first country to adopt the Pan-African colours after they had been initiated by Ethiopia (*q.v.*); their order in the modern flag accords with that in the original Ethiopian version. The flag was adopted on Ghana's attaining independence in 1957, dropped in 1964 when the country became a one-party state – the yellow being replaced by white to match the flag of that one party, the Convention People's Party – and reintroduced in 1966. The black star represents both the people of Ghana and the cause of African unity and liberty.

POPULATION: 14,200,000
CAPITAL: Accra
AREA: 92,000 sq mi (238,500 km^2)
LANGUAGES: English, Akan, Ewe, Ga
RELIGIONS: Christianity, indigenous religions, Islam

GREECE
The Hellenic Republic

The Greek flag has been inspired by the Stars and Stripes, with the stripes representing the nine syllables of the freedom slogan used in the war for independence from the Ottomans during 1821–32; the cross has Christian meanings that vary according to interpretation. Blue is for the sea and sky, white for the purity of the freedom fighters' cause. The shade of blue has been altered from time to time. Before 1970 the modern flag was, in general, flown at sea; between 1970 and 1974 only the striped flag was used; in 1974–5 the two flags were used as previously; from 1975 to 1978 only the cross flag was officially used; and finally, in 1978, the current design was established as the sole national flag.

POPULATION: 10,000,000
CAPITAL: Athens (Athínai)
AREA: 51,000 sq mi (132,000 km^2)
LANGUAGE: Greek
RELIGION: Christianity (almost exclusively Greek Orthodox)

GRENADA

The flag of Grenada was adopted on the attainment of independence from the UK in 1974 and has remained unchanged. Set within the triangle to the left of centre is a stylized nutmeg, acknowledging the importance of the spice to the nation's economy. The green of the flag represents vegetal richness, the red has its customary implications of vitality, determination and liberation and the yellow is for sunshine, friendliness and wisdom. There are seven stars for the nation's seven parishes, one of which comprises those few of the Grenadine Islands that are not part of St Vincent and The Grenadines (*q.v.*); the star-shape itself expresses optimism and idealism.

POPULATION: 104,000
CAPITAL: St George's
AREA: 133 sq mi (345 km^2)
LANGUAGES: English, French
RELIGION: Christianity

GUATEMALA
The Republic of Guatemala

Until 1821 Guatemala was part of the captaincy-general of Guatemala, which was ruled by Spain; in this year the captaincy-general as a whole declared independence, but was almost immediately swallowed up by the Mexican Empire. By 1824 Guatemala, Costa Rica, El Salvador, Honduras and Nicaragua – had regained their freedom and formed the Central American Federation, an arrangement that was soon to be unravelled, in 1838. The flag of the CAF was a simple blue and white triband, and it was to this design that Guatemala turned. Between 1851 and 1871 there were additional stripes of yellow and red; when these disappeared and the country reverted to the simple blue and white, the stripes were set vertically.

POPULATION: 8,700,000
CAPITAL: Guatemala City
AREA: 42,000 sq mi (109,000 km^2)
LANGUAGES: Spanish, indigenous languages
RELIGIONS: Christianity (mainly RC), indigenous religions

GUINEA
The Republic of Guinea

The flag of Guinea, introduced a few weeks after independence in 1958, has the design of the French tricolour but using the Pan-African colours. These were adopted in imitation not of Ethiopia (*q.v.*) but of Ghana (*q.v.*), it being at the time the aim of the two countries to unite. The national motto is *Travail, Justice, Solidarité* ("Work, Justice, Solidarity"), and the red, yellow and green of the flag are sometimes taken to represent these three qualities respectively.

POPULATION: 5,100,000
CAPITAL: Conakry
AREA: 95,000 sq mi (246,000 km^2)
LANGUAGES: French, indigenous languages
RELIGIONS: Islam, indigenous religions

GUINEA-BISSAU
The Republic of Guinea-Bissau

The flag depicts the Pan-African colours of red, yellow and green and the black five-pointed star symbolizing African freedom. Similar to the earlier flag of Cape Verde, this is explained by the fact that both are derived from that of the Partido Africano da Independencia da Guiné e Cabo Verde (PAIGC; African Party for the Independence of Guinea and Cape Verde), the liberation movement that succeeded in gaining independence for both countries (Guinea-Bissau in 1974, Cape Verde in 1975). PAIGC's aim had been that the two nations should unite, and this merger was well under way when scotched in 1980 by a military coup in Guinea-Bissau. Cape Verde adopted a new flag in 1992.

POPULATION: 945,000
CAPITAL: Bissau
AREA: 13,900 sq mi (36,125 km^2)
LANGUAGES: Portuguese, Creole, indigenous languages
RELIGIONS: indigenous religions, Islam (Christian minority)

GUYANA
The Co-operative Republic of Guyana

The flag of Guyana was adopted on the country's attainment of independence from the UK in 1966; it was based on a design supplied by Dr Whitney Smith (1940–), Director of the Flag Research Center at Winchester, Massachusetts. Dr Smith has explained it as follows: "The red triangle stands for the people's zeal in nation building; its black border is for endurance. The gold arrowhead represents progress and the nation's mineral wealth; its white border is for the rivers of Guyana. The green field represents farms and forests."

The flag of the President of Guyana

POPULATION: 1,000,000
CAPITAL: Georgetown
AREA: 83,000 sq mi (215,000 km^2)
LANGUAGES: English, Hindi, Creole
RELIGIONS: Christianity, Hinduism, Islam

HAITI
The Republic of Haiti

The first flag of Haiti was the French tricolour. On independence in 1804 Jean Jacques Dessalines (1758–1806) became emperor and adopted a bi-colour national flag disposing of the white, with the blue being replaced by black. In 1806 Dessalines was assassinated and the new president reintroduced blue and red. In 1818, the pattern of two horizontal bands in blue and in red was adopted and from 1844 the arms, in a rectangular white frame, were added. In 1964, when François Duvalier (1907–71), declared himself president for life, the flag was altered back to the Dessalines pattern, although the arms were retained. After Duvalier died in 1971 the pre-Duvalier blue and red flag was reintroduced, and is still the national flag.

POPULATION: 5,500,000
CAPITAL: Port-au-Prince
AREA: 10,710 sq mi (27,750 km^2)
LANGUAGES: French, Creole
RELIGIONS: Christianity (mainly RC), Voodoo

HONDURAS
The Republic of Honduras

POPULATION: 4,800,000
CAPITAL: Tegucigalpa
AREA: 43,250 sq mi (112,000 km²)
LANGUAGES: Spanish, indigenous languages
RELIGION: Christianity (almost exclusively RC)

Until 1821 Honduras was part of the captaincy-general of Guatemala, which was ruled by Spain; in that year the captaincy-general as a whole declared independence but was almost immediately swallowed up by the Mexican Empire. By 1824 Honduras, Costa Rica, El Salvador, Guatemala and Nicaragua – had regained their freedom and formed the Central American Federation, an arrangement that was soon to be unravelled, in 1838. The flag of the CAF was a simple blue and white triband, and it was to this design that Honduras turned, adding the five stars for the five CAF countries in 1866 (although not ratified until 1949). On the state flag the stars are arranged into an arc, to accommodate the presence of the arms.

HUNGARY
The Republic of Hungary

POPULATION: 10,600,000
CAPITAL: Budapest
AREA: 36,000 sq mi (93,000 km²)
LANGUAGE: Magyar
RELIGION: Christianity

The red, white and green colours of Hungary are thought to date back to the 9th century; a precursor of the modern flag was used by King Matthias II (1557–1619), later (from 1612) Holy Roman Emperor. In 1848 the Hungarians, led by Lajos (Louis) Kossuth (1802–94), rebelled against Austrian rule and gained short-lived independence in 1849, with Kossuth as governor; he used the traditional colours in the pattern of the French tricolour, and this was thereafter the national flag with the addition of the arms, until 1945 and the declaration of a new republic. When the communists took over in 1949 they added their emblem to the flag; this was dropped in 1956 around the time of the Hungarian uprising and its brutal suppression by Soviet troops.

ICELAND
The Republic of Iceland

POPULATION: 250,000
CAPITAL: Reykjavik
AREA: 39,700 sq mi (103,000 km²)
LANGUAGE: Icelandic
RELIGION: Christianity (almost exclusively Evangelical Lutheran)

Iceland uses a version of the Scandinavian Cross, seen also in the flags of Denmark (*q.v.*), Finland, Norway and Sweden (*qq.v.*). In the Icelandic version the colours reflect those of Denmark – which ruled the country 1381–1918 and of which Iceland was then an independent state until independence in 1944 – and of Norway, which ruled Iceland from 1264 until both came under the Danish crown in 1381. The Icelandic flag was adopted in 1915, but only for home waters until 1918.

INDIA
The Republic of India

The Indian flag is very similar to that of the Indian National Congress party, from which it was directly derived. The Congress flag was first used with the colours saffron (courage and sacrifice), green (faith, fertility and chivalry) and white (truth and peace) in 1933; in the centre of the white band was the emblem of a spinning-wheel. On independence the spinning-wheel was replaced by the image of a Buddhist *dharma chakra* (wheel of life), which had recently been discovered at Sarnath on a column dating from the time of the Indian Emperor Ashoka (reigned 269–232BC), who was converted to Buddhism and established it as the state religion.

POPULATION: 813,000,000
CAPITAL: New Delhi
AREA: 1,270,000 sq mi (3,288,000 km²)
LANGUAGES: Hindi, English, Urdu and many others
RELIGIONS: Hinduism, Islam (Sikh, Christian, Buddhist and Jain minorities)

INDONESIA
The Republic of Indonesia

Immediately after World War II, Indonesia unilaterally declared her independence from her Dutch overlords, a decision finally ratified four years later, in 1949. The national flag dates from the initial declaration of independence, its status having been confirmed in 1949. Before that it had been used from about 1924 by Indonesian freedom fighters in their struggle against the Dutch, but the use of the colours can be traced back to the 13th century. The white is, as ever, for purity and justice; the red is for gallantry and freedom. Except in its proportions, the flag is identical with the venerable flag of Monaco (*q.v.*).

POPULATION: 175,000,000
CAPITAL: Jakarta (Djakarta)
AREA: 782,500 sq mi (2,030,000 km²)
LANGUAGE: Bahasa Indonesian
RELIGIONS: Islam, Christianity (Hindu and Buddhist minorities)

IRAN
The Islamic Republic of Iran

The current form of the Iranian flag was adopted after 1979 when an Islamic republic was declared with the return to eminence of the Ayatollah Ruhollah Khomeini (1900–89). The colours of the flag, adopted in 1907, are traditional, having been used on Iranian flags since at least the 18th century. The central emblem – a sword with beckoning crescents – was confirmed shortly after Iran's 1979 declaration of herself as a republic; it expresses Islamic values. Along the edges of both the red and green bands the expression *Allah o Akbar* ("God is Great") is repeated 22 times; this inscription marks the return of Khomeini to Iran on the 22nd day of the Islamic month of Bahman. Note the curious notched effect along the borders of the white stripe.

POPULATION: 52,500,000
CAPITAL: Tehran (Teheran)
AREA: 636,300 sq mi (1,648,000 km²)
LANGUAGES: Farsi, Kurdish, Baluchi
RELIGION: Islam

IRAQ
The Republic of Iraq

Like that of Jordan (*q.v.*) and others, the flag of Iraq is in the Pan-Arab colours; indeed, before 1958 the Iraqi flag was hard to tell from the Jordanian, the only differences being that the red area was a trapezium rather than a triangle and that there were two white stars rather than one within this area. A different flag was used between 1958 (when the monarchy was ousted) and 1963, when the current flag was adopted, the three green stars representing the unfulfilled expectation of coming together in political union with Egypt and Syria. Since the Gulf War of 1991, when both Egypt and Syria played an active part in the UN force that drove Iraq back out of Kuwait, such union has seemed even more remote than before.

POPULATION: 17,000,000
CAPITAL: Baghdad
AREA: 168,000 sq mi (435,000 km²)
LANGUAGES: Arabic, Kurdish, Turkish, Assyrian
RELIGIONS: Islam, Christianity

IRISH REPUBLIC
The Republic of Ireland

The colour scheme of the Irish flag is easily explained: the green is for the Catholics, the orange for the Protestants and the white for the need for peace and unity between the two. Although the colours had been used before in this way, the first significant occasion of their use was in the wake of the revolutions that swept Europe in 1848 against post-Napoleonic conservatism, resulting notably in the ousting of the French King Louis-Philippe. Even so, it was not until the 1916 uprising that the use of the colours to symbolize a free and united Ireland became widespread. The colours were adopted in 1919, and their modern arrangement was finalized in 1920; the Free State was established in 1921. The flag has remained unchanged since.

POPULATION: 3,540,000
CAPITAL: Dublin (Baile Atha Cliath)
AREA: 27,000 sq mi (70,300 km²)
LANGUAGES: English, Erse
RELIGIONS: Christianity (almost exclusively RC)

ISRAEL
The State of Israel

Israel has had the same flag since the state was formed in 1948. The flag itself dates back to the early days of the Zionist movement, being introduced in 1891 and confirmed in 1897 by the First Zionist Congress, when the movement also established the World Zionist Organization and appointed its leading light, the Hungarian-born journalist and playwright Theodor Herzl (1860–1904), as its first president. The emblem in the centre of the flag is the Star (or Shield) of David, a six-pointed star composed of two equilateral triangles, a centuries-old Jewish symbol. Blue and white are traditional colours for ritual cloths, most especially prayer shawls, the blue stripes around the edges of which are referred to by the blue stripes in the flag.

POPULATION: 4,480,000
CAPITAL: Jerusalem (Yerushalayim)
AREA: 8,000 sq mi (21,000 km²)
LANGUAGES: Hebrew, Arabic
RELIGIONS: Judaism, Islam

ITALY
The Italian Republic

The Italian tricolour is the French tricolour but with green in place of blue. According to one legend, the change was effected because green was Napoleon's favourite colour. It first appeared in the French republics in northern Italy set up in the late 18th century, being adopted in 1797–8 by the Cisalpine Republic. In 1802 it became the flag of the Italian republic that the French had set up, and it endured until 1814. In 1848 the green-white-red tricolour was adopted, with the arms of the House of Savoy in the centre. In 1946, when Italy proclaimed itself a republic in the wake of World War II – its last king, Umberto II (1904–) having abdicated following a referendum that rejected the monarchy – the arms of the House of Savoy were removed.

POPULATION: 57,500,000
CAPITAL: Rome (Roma)
AREA: 116,300 sq mi (301,225 km^2)
LANGUAGE: Italian
RELIGION: Christianity (mainly RC)

IVORY COAST
The Republic of Côte d'Ivoire

The flag of the Ivory Coast (or, since 1986, officially Côte d'Ivoire) was adopted in 1959, the year before the country gained its independence from France. Unlike most other ex-colonies, it decided to express in its flag its continuing relationship with its one-time ruler, adopting the pattern of the French tricolour. The sharing of colours with Ireland (*q.v.*) is coincidental. The orange is for the Ivory Coast's northern savannas, the green for its lush coastal regions and the white for the harmony and unity of the peoples of these two areas.

POPULATION: 11,600,000
CAPITALS: Abidjan/Yamoussoukro
AREA: 125,000 sq mi (322,500 km^2)
LANGUAGES: French, indigenous languages including Dioula
RELIGIONS: Animism, Islam, Christianity

JAMAICA

The flag of Jamaica was introduced on independence in 1962 and has remained unchanged. The design appears to have been inspired purely by aesthetics. The colours are interpreted as follows: yellow for mineral resources and for sunshine, green for agricultural wealth and for hope, and black for the hardships that the nation's people have faced in the past (notably slavery) and still continue to face.

The arms of Jamaica

POPULATION: 2,400,000
CAPITAL: Kingston
AREA: 4250 sq mi (11,000 km^2)
LANGUAGE: English
RELIGIONS: Christianity, Rastafarianism

JAPAN

Japan's name means "The Land of the Rising Sun", and its emperors claim direct descent from the sun goddess, so it is not surprising that the red disc of the sun should be the central image of the national flag; what *is* surprising is that this been so only since 1870 – although it had been put to mercantile use for a number of years before that, and the symbol and its imperial connections date back a further 500 years. The redness of the disc expresses qualities such as sincerity and passion, the whiteness of the background honesty and purity.

POPULATION: 122,600,000
CAPITAL: Tokyo
AREA: 143,700 sq mi (372,000 km^2)
LANGUAGE: Japanese
RELIGIONS: Shintoism, Buddhism

JORDAN
The Hashemite Kingdom of Jordan

The seven-pointed star added in 1928 to Jordan's flag created in 1921, represents the seven verses of the Koran's first *sura*, "The Opening" (*al-Fatiha*), which is held by many Islamic divines to comprehend all the essentials of their belief. The colours derive from that of the kingdom of Hejaz (now a part of Saudi Arabia), within whose domain lay Mecca. Before Jordan became an independent kingdom (1946) it was controlled by the UK under a League of Nations mandate; the drive for liberation was inspired by Hussein ibn Ali (1856–1931), King of Hejaz, and his colours (red, white, green and black) were widely used, becoming known as the Pan-Arab colours and now adopted by a number of other Arab countries

POPULATION: 3,940,000
CAPITAL: Amman
AREA: 37,750 sq mi (97,750 km^2)
LANGUAGE: Arabic
RELIGION: Islam (Christianity minority)

KAZAKHSTAN
The Republic of Kazakhstan

Kazakhstan has been a unitary state since 1991, having become so at the time of the general dissolution of the Union of Soviet Socialist Republics. About 100 nationalities are represented in the Kazakhstani population, of whom only about one-third are native Kazakhs, adherents of Islam noted for their skill in horsemanship; most of the remaining people are either Russian or Ukrainian. The region became a part of Russia progressively through the 18th and 19th centuries; traditionally there has been rivalry over the border it shares with northwestern China. Kazakhstan's flag was designed in 1992; the central feature is a shining sun and a soaring eagle of the Steppes, against the sky. In the hoist is a golden "traditional national ornament".

POPULATION: 15,858,000
CAPITAL: Alma-Ata
AREA: 1,049,150 sq mi (2,717,300 km^2)
LANGUAGES: Russian, Ukrainian, Kazakh
RELIGIONS: Christianity, Islam

KENYA
The Republic of Kenya

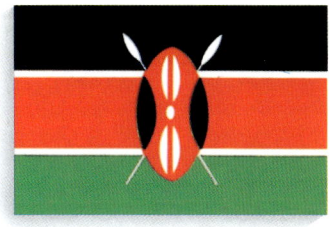

The current Kenyan flag, adopted on the country's attainment of independence from the UK in 1963, is based on that adopted in 1952 by the leading political party, the Kenya African National Union (KANU); for the national flag the central image of the shield with crossed spears was elaborated and, more significantly, white stripes were added as a recognition of Kenya's other main political party, the Kenya African Democratic Union (KADU), which was soon absorbed by KANU as Kenya became a one-party state under Jomo Kenyatta (c1891–1978), first President of Kenya from 1964 until his death. The white implies peace and unity, the colours are those used elsewhere to express the Black liberation struggle.

POPULATION: 23,900,000
CAPITAL: Nairobi
AREA: 225,000 sq mi (583,000 km^2)
LANGUAGES: Swahili, English
RELIGIONS: Christianity, indigenous religions (Islamic minority)

KIRIBATI
The Republic of Kiribati

Before independence in 1979, the Gilbert Islands (as Kiribati then was) flew the British Blue Ensign with the shield from the arms of the Gilbert and Ellice Islands Protectorate, as did the Ellice Islands, now Tuvalu (*q.v.*), from which the Gilberts had been partitioned in 1975. Those arms had been granted in 1937; they showed a yellow frigate bird above a sun rising over the Pacific Ocean, and the Kiribati flag – chosen as the winner of a design competition – was drawn almost directly from them.

The arms of Kiribati

POPULATION: 66,250
CAPITAL: Tarawa
AREA: 264 sq mi (680 km^2)
LANGUAGES: Gilbertese, English
RELIGION: Christianity

KOREA (North)
The Democratic People's Republic of Korea

The whole of the ancient kingdom of Korea became a Japanese protectorate in 1905 and was formally annexed by Japan in 1910. After World War II the country was divided by the Allies at the 38th parallel, the north being allotted to the USSR and the south to the USA. In 1948 the north became an independent "democratic people's republic" i.e., a communist state. The traditional Korean flag was in the colours red, white and blue. The communist regime of the north retained these colours and incorporated a red star in a white disc; an expression of the glorious future that communism would bring. White is for purity and the sovereignty of the nation, while blue is the desire for peace – that endured until 1950.

POPULATION: 22,000,000
CAPITAL: Pyongyang (Pyeongyang)
AREA: 47,350 sq mi (122,600 km^2)
LANGUAGE: Korean
RELIGIONS: Shamanism, Chundo Kyo, Buddhism

KOREA (South)
The Republic of Korea

In 1948 when Korea was divided up the south was established as a democracy. The traditional Korean flag was in the colours red, white and blue, and a version of it adopted in the 1880s was reintroduced in 1948, with minor adjustments, in 1950 as the flag of the south. The central feature is the yin-yang symbol, which has its customary Buddhist fusion-of-opposites meaning, stressed also by the choice of the colours red and blue. The white background expresses purity. The meanings of the four black trigrams fall into three sequences. Reading in each case clockwise from upper left, these are: summer, autumn, winter, spring; south, west, north, east; sky (heaven), moon, Earth, sun.

POPULATION: 22,000,000
CAPITAL: Pyongyang (Pyeongyang)
AREA: 47,350 sq mi (122,600 km²)
LANGUAGE: Korean
RELIGIONS: Shamanism, Chundo Kyo, Buddhism

KUWAIT
The State of Kuwait

Like that of Jordan (*q.v.*) and others, the Kuwaiti flag is in the Pan-Arab colours of red, white, green and black. The flag was adopted in 1961, when Kuwait gained its independence from the UK, of which it had been a protectorate since 1914. There are various interpretations of the colours: red may be the blood of enemies, courage or a representation of the Hashemites; white may be purity, peace, honour or a representation of the Umayyads; green may be agriculture, vegetation or a representation of the Fatimids; and black may be colour of the future for the state's foes, the stained mud kicked up by horses in battle or a representation of the Abbasids.

POPULATION: 2,000,000
CAPITAL: Kuwait City (Al-Kuwayt)
AREA: 6875 sq mi (17,800 km²)
LANGUAGES: Arabic, English
RELIGION: Islam

KYRGYZSTAN
The Republic of Kyrgyzstan

Kyrgyzstan has been a unitary state since 1991, having become so at the time of the general dissolution of the Union of Soviet Socialist Republics. Traditionally there has been rivalry over its border with northwestern China, where rise the vast peaks of the Tien Shan Range. There are strong links with the neighbouring, and much larger, state of Kazakhstan. The flag, adopted in 1992, features a bird's-eye view of a yurt, a traditional felt tent, with criss-crossed ropes to hold it down. It is surrounded by 40 golden rays representing the 40 traditional tribes of Kyrgyzstan.

POPULATION: 3,976,000
CAPITAL: Bishket
AREA: 76,640 sq mi (198,500 km²)
LANGUAGES: Kyrgyz, Turkish, Russian
RELIGION: Islam

LAOS
The Lao People's Democratic Republic

In 1954 Laos attained its full independence from the French, but the country remained a constitutional monarchy (as it had been since 1947); at the time of independence it was already in the grip of a vicious civil war, begun in 1953, between the existing government and the communist-led and Vietnam-assisted Neo Lao Istala. In 1975 the Neo Lao Istala took power and declared The Lao People's Democratic Republic. The new national flag was identical with that adopted in 1945 and depicts a white (for justice and the promise of the future) full moon superimposed on a blue (for the people's well-being) Mekong River flanked on either side by red (for the unity and purpose of the Laotians and for the blood they shed during the struggle for freedom).

POPULATION: 3,900,000
CAPITAL: Vientiane (Viangchan)
AREA: 91,400 sq mi (236,750 km^2)
LANGUAGES: Lao, indigenous languages
RELIGIONS: Buddhism, indigenous religions, Christianity

LATVIA
The Republic of Latvia

Latvia has been a unitary state since 1991, having become so at the time of the general dissolution of the Union of Soviet Socialist Republics; before that, since its annexation by the USSR in 1944, it was regarded by the USA and a few other Western governments as being illegally occupied. Its earlier history is virtually a string of occupations by some foreign power or another: the Vikings, Denmark, Lithuania, Germany, Poland, Sweden, Russia and the USSR – although it did have a shaky period of independence from 1920 until Russia invaded in 1940 and then Germany in 1941–4. The majority of the people are of the Letts, an ancient Baltic people, but about one-third are Russians.

POPULATION: 2,681,000
CAPITAL: Riga
AREA: 24,580 sq mi (63,700 km^2)
LANGUAGES: Lettish, Russian, many others
RELIGION: Lutheran Christianity

LEBANON
The Lebanese Republic

The cedar tree has been a Lebanese symbol since Biblical times; its use on a white flag appears to date from the 18th century, when the Maronite Christians of Lebanon adopted the symbol, and certainly it appeared on a flag of 1861. When the country came under French mandate in 1920 the flag used was the French tricolour with the cedar tree in the central stripe. In 1943, a few weeks before Lebanon became independent on 1 January 1944, the current version was adopted as the national flag.

Lebanon's flag of the sea

POPULATION: 2,600,000
CAPITAL: Beirut
AREA: 4,000 sq mi (10,360 km^2)
LANGUAGES: Arabic, French, English
RELIGIONS: Islam, Christianity

LESOTHO
The Kingdom of Lesotho

The current Lesotho flag dates only from 1986, when a coup ousted the ruling Lesotho National Party, whose colours had previously been used for the flag since independence in 1966. The image of the shield with crossed spear and war-club symbolizes the will of the people to defend their nation. The flag also has white for peace, blue for rain and green for prosperity.

The Royal Standard of Lesotho

POPULATION: 1,700,000
CAPITAL: Maseru
AREA: 11,700 sq mi (30,350 km²)
LANGUAGES: Sesotho, English
RELIGIONS: Christianity, indigenous religions

LIBERIA
The Republic of Liberia

The national flag of Liberia, adopted on the country's becoming the first independent Black African republic in 1847, is modelled on the Stars and Stripes; this is hardly coincidental, since it was largely as a result of the American Colonization Society, that freed slaves from the USA were able to return to the territory that is now Liberia. A similar flag had been used since 1827, but it had 13 stripes and, in place of the star, a white cross – expressing Liberia as a colony of the USA, and the Christian inspiration of the American Colonization Society. The current 11 stripes of the flag denote the 11 signatures on Liberia's Declaration of Independence; the star is for the shining light in darkness that the new country was intended to represent.

POPULATION: 2,500,000
CAPITAL: Monrovia
AREA: 43,000 sq mi (110,000 km²)
LANGUAGES: English, indigenous languages
RELIGIONS: indigenous religions, Islam, Christianity

LIBYA
The Great Socialist People's Libyan Arab Jamahiriya

In 1971 Libya adopted the flag of the Federation of Arab Republics, but in 1977, after (possibly government inspired) scenes of rioting and flag-burning in the streets over the decision of Egypt (*q.v.*). one of the federation's other two members, to seek peace with Israel, the current national flag was adopted. This is in plain green to denote the nation's complete devotion to Islam and also the agricultural ("green") revolution dictated by the Libyan leader since a military coup and the abolition of the monarchy in 1969.

POPULATION: 4,230,000
CAPITAL: Tripoli (Tarabulus)
AREA: 680,000 sq mi (1,760,000 km²)
LANGUAGE: Arabic
RELIGION: Islam

LIECHTENSTEIN
The Principality of Liechtenstein

The red and blue of the Liechtenstein flag date back to the early 19th century, and in 1921 the principality adopted them in a straightforward bicolour. One of the less significant political upheavals consequent upon the 1936 Olympic Games in Berlin – "Hitler's Games" – was a result of the discovery that Haiti (*q.v.*) and Leichtenstein had extremely similar flags. Liechtenstein therefore added in 1937 the yellow coronet both to avoid confusion and to indicate the country's status as a principality.

The arms of Liechtenstein

POPULATION: 28,500
CAPITAL: Vaduz
AREA: 62 sq mi (160 km²)
LANGUAGES: German, Alemannic
RELIGION: Christianity (mainly RC)

LITHUANIA
The Republic of Lithuania

Lithuania has been a unitary state since 1991, having become so at the time of the general dissolution of the Union of Soviet Socialist Republics. The region, then including much of what is today Ukraine (*q.v.*) was settled by the Lithuanian people before the 12th century, becoming part of the Polish-Lithuanian Empire, which was progressively depleted by the assaults of Germany, Sweden and Russia; by the end of the 18th century Lithuania was a province of the latter. From 1918–1940 Lithuania was independent; then it was occupied by Russia, followed by Germany in 1941–4. Its annexation by the USSR in 1944 was regarded by some Western governments as an illegal occupation, so that they continued to recognize Lithuania as a nation.

POPULATION: 3,690,000
CAPITAL: Vilnius
AREA: 25,200 sq mi (65,200 km²)
LANGUAGES: Lithuanian, Russian, Lettish
RELIGION: Roman Catholicism

LUXEMBOURG
The Grand Duchy of Luxembourg

The flag of Luxembourg is hard to distinguish from that of The Netherlands (*q.v.*); this is partly a consequence of the fact that Luxembourg shared a common dynasty with The Netherlands; the House of Orange. In fact, the Luxembourgian use of the colours dates back to the 13th century, and possibly earlier. From 1845 to 1890 the two flags were identical, after which Luxembourg opted to use a much paler shade of blue and a more elongated shape.

POPULATION: 377,500
CAPITAL: Luxembourg
AREA: 1,000 sq mi (2,600 km²)
LANGUAGES: Letzeburghish, French, German, English
RELIGION: Christianity (mainly RC)

MADAGASCAR
The Republic of Madagascar

Madagascar became a French protectorate in 1896; it gained autonomy within the French Community in 1958, when it took the name of the Malagasy Republic (which it retained until 1975) and adopted its current flag. Much of the ancestry of the people derives less from Africa than from southeast Asia – and two of the colours of the flag may likewise owe their origins to the more distant continent. These are red and white, the traditional colours used in the flags of the Merina (Hova) people of Madagascar's central plateau, the largest single tribal group, and ruled the country until the French conquest. The green is for the coastal people, the Betsimisaraka, who have ruled since independence.

POPULATION: 11,250,000
CAPITAL: Antananarivo (Tananarive)
AREA: 226,600 sq mi (587,000 km²)
LANGUAGES: Malagasy, French
RELIGIONS: indigenous religions, Christianity

MALAWI

The Malawi national flag, adopted on the country's attainment of independence from the UK in 1964, was based on the tricolour adopted in 1953 by the principal political party involved in the struggle for the freedom of the then Nyasaland, the Malawi Congress Party, which took power when its aim was realized; in 1966 Malawi became a one-party republic with Hastings Banda (1905–   ) as president (declared president for life in 1971). The sole revision when the tricolour was adopted as the national flag was the introduction in the black band of a red dawning sun to symbolize the new era. The colours are those of the Black Liberation Movement.

POPULATION: 7,750,000
CAPITAL: Lilongwe
AREA: 45,750 sq mi (118,500 km²)
LANGUAGES: Chichewa, English
RELIGIONS: Christianity, indigenous religions, Islam

MALAYSIA

Malaysia, formed in 1963, and consisted of the 11 states of the previous Federation of Malaya plus Singapore (*q.v.*), the northern Borneo states of Sarawak and Sabah. The original Malayan flag adopted in 1950 had been inspired by the Stars and Stripes, had 11 stripes, and the large yellow star had 11 points, in recognition of the 11 states. When Malaysia was formed, the number of both stripes and points was simply increased to 14, and that number was retained even after Singapore's secession in 1965, the "extra" stripe representing the nation's capital, Kuala Lumpur. The star and crescent are Islamic symbols, the red and white are traditional colours, the yellow represents states that are sultanates, and the blue reflects the long history of the British in Malaya.

POPULATION: 17,000,000
CAPITAL: Kuala Lumpur
AREA: 127,500 sq mi (330,000 km²)
LANGUAGES: Malay, Chinese, Tamil, English, indigenous languages
RELIGIONS: Islam, Buddhism (Hindu and Christian minorities)

MALDIVES
The Republic of Maldives

The national flag of Maldives was adopted in 1965 when the country gained its independence from the UK. At the start of the 20th century the flag had been plain red, reflecting the culture of the numerous Arab traders who operated among the many islands of the chain. Their influence is apparent also in the later addition of a rectangle in Islamic green containing a crescent.

The arms of the Maldives

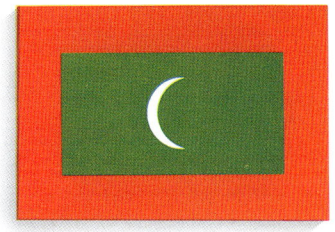

POPULATION: 202,000
CAPITAL: Malé
AREA: 115 sq mi (300 km^2)
LANGUAGES: Divehi (Sinhalese), English
RELIGION: Islam

MALI
The Republic of Mali

In 1960 Mali and Senegal (*q.v.*) became independent together, having in the previous year federated – to form the Federation of Mali – and adopted a joint flag; shortly after independence the two nations agreed to go their separate ways, Mali keeping both name and flag. This was a tricolour in the Pan-African colours with a black human figure – the kanaga, expressing black consciousness – limed in the central yellow stripe. Not surprisingly, however, the largely Islamic population of the country protested at this depiction of the human form, and in 1961 it was dropped from the flag, thereby causing problems for Rwanda (*q.v.*), whose flag was then identical with Mali's.

POPULATION: 8,900,000
CAPITAL: Bamako
AREA: 480,000 sq mi (1,240,000 km^2)
LANGUAGES: French, indigenous languages
RELIGIONS: Islam, Animism

MALTA
The Republic of Malta

The national flag of Malta dates from 1964 when the island gained its independence from the UK. The red and white dates back much further, having its origins in the various flags used in Malta showing, on a red background, a white Cross of the Order of the Knights of St John (the "Maltese Cross"), the organization that had ruled the island from 1530 until 1798. In 1942 George VI of the UK (1895–1952) awarded the George Cross to the population of Malta, and this was commemorated by the addition to the flag of the cross on a square blue background. On independence the blue square was replaced by a thin red border.

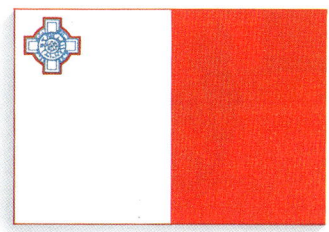

POPULATION: 345,600
CAPITAL: Valletta
AREA: 122 sq mi (315 km^2)
LANGUAGES: Maltese, English
RELIGION: Christianity (almost exclusively RC)

MARSHALL ISLANDS
The Republic of the Marshall Islands

The Marshall Islands were a German protectorate from 1899, captured and occupied by Japan during World War I, taken by the USA during World War II. They became self-governing in 1979 and finally became an independent republic in free association with the USA in 1986, an association that may surprise, since the US tested 64 nuclear bombs at Bikini and Enewetak in the Marshalls between 1946 and 1958. The current flag dates from 1979. The blue is for the Pacific Ocean, the orange-red for courage and prosperity, and the white for brightness. The four larger rays of the star are for Majuro (the capital) and the three administrative districts; the 20 shorter ones are for the nation's municipalities.

POPULATION: 40,100
CAPITAL: Majuro
AREA: 70 sq mi (180 km^2)
LANGUAGES: Marshallese, English
RELIGION: Christianity

MAURITANIA
The Islamic Republic of Mauritania

The Islamic allegiances of Mauritania can hardly be in doubt: the green of her flag as well as the symbol, in yellow, of the crescent with five-pointed star tell the whole story. Mauritania, originally part of French West Africa, gained autonomy within the French Community in 1958 and adopted this flag in 1959, remaining loyal to it on attaining full independence in 1960.

POPULATION: 1,900,000
CAPITAL: Nouakchott
AREA: 400,000 sq mi (1,031,000 km^2)
LANGUAGES: Arabic, French, indigenous languages
RELIGION: Islam

MAURITIUS
The Republic of Mauritius

The current flag of Mauritius was adopted in 1968 at the time the nation attained its independence. Its colours – red, blue, yellow and green – are those of the coat of arms adopted in 1906. Meanings have been ascribed to the colours since 1968: the red is for the liberation struggle and for the blood spilled in the course of this struggle, the blue is for the Indian Ocean, the yellow is for the sunlight of freedom and for the bright future, and the green is for agriculture and for the all-year-round vegetation of the country.

POPULATION: 1,078,000
CAPITAL: Port Louis
AREA: 790 sq mi (2,040 km^2)
LANGUAGES: English, French, Creole, Hindi
RELIGIONS: Christianity (almost exclusively RC), Hinduism, Islam

MEXICO
The United Mexican States

The green, white and red tricolour of Mexico was introduced in 1821, around the time that the country gained its independence; a couple of years later, in 1823, the flag was established with the three stripes arranged vertically and with the country's arms as an emblem in the centre of the white stripe. The arms have undergone many changes since 1823 (the latest version, 1968), but have always shown an eagle eating a snake while perched atop a cactus on an island in a lake. This symbol dates back to the Aztecs, whose legend of the founding of their nation was that their nomadic ancestors were told that they should live at a place where they came across such a scene. This they did in 1325, on the site of what is now Mexico City.

POPULATION: 83,000,000
CAPITAL: Mexico City
AREA: 761,700 sq mi (1,973,000 km^2)
LANGUAGES: Spanish, indigenous languages
RELIGION: Christianity (almost exclusively RC)

MICRONESIA
The Federated States of Micronesia

A federated state in free association with the USA, Micronesia was earlier part of the UN Trust Territory of the Pacific Islands, administered by the USA; she gained her present status in 1985. The first flag for Micronesia was introduced in 1962: it was in the UN colours of pale blue and white, and showed six stars representing the six states that were then a part of the federation. In 1978 the current form of the flag, with four stars to show that there were now only four states, was introduced, and it has remained in use since. Of these four states – Kosrae, Pohnpei, Truk and Yap – Pohnpei, on which stands the capital, Kolonia, accounts for more than 50 per cent of the land area.

POPULATION: 86,000
CAPITAL: Kolonia
AREA: 280 sq mi (720 km^2)
LANGUAGES: English, indigenous languages
RELIGION: Christianity (mainly RC)

MOLDOVA
The Republic of Moldova

Moldova has been a unitary state since 1991, having become so at the time of the general dissolution of the Union of Soviet Socialist Republics. The historical region of Moldova is today divided by the Prut River, so that part of it lies in Romania. Between the Prut and the Dniester lies that part of Moldova called Bessarabia; this was ceded to Russia in 1812, became part of Moldavia in 1856, was regained by Russia in 1878, controlled (1918–44) by Romania and then finally became a part of the Moldavian and Ukrainian SSRs. The colours of the flag, adopted in 1990, reflect the flag of Romania, a country to which the inhabitants are ethnically and linguistically related. In the centre is an eagle bearing a stylised version of the shield of Moldova.

POPULATION: 4,341,000
CAPITAL: Kishinev (Kisin'ov)
AREA: 13,000 sq mi (33,700 km^2)
LANGUAGES: Russian, Romanian
RELIGION: Christianity

MONACO
The Principality of Monaco

Except for the proportions, the flag of Monaco is identical with that of Indonesia – a fact about which Monaco has complained on numerous occasions since 1945, when the current Indonesian flag was introduced (officially confirmed 1949). And with some justice, for Monaco's claim is of considerably greater antiquity. Although the flag itself was adopted in its current form only as "recently" as 1881, its colours date back to the 14th century, when they were established by the House of Grimaldi, which has ruled since 1297.

POPULATION: 28,000
CAPITAL: Monaco-Ville
AREA: 0.76 sq mi (1.95 km²)
LANGUAGES: French, Monégasque
RELIGION: Christianity (mainly RC)

The arms of Monaco

MONGOLIA
The Mongolian People's Republic

Mongolia was one of the very first communist states, abolishing its monarchy and declaring itself as a people's republic as early as 1924. In 1946 Mongolia's independence was guaranteed by the Sino-Soviet treaty. The current flag dates from a few years earlier, 1940, is socialist red with blue to symbolize the sky and thereby the Mongol people; beneath the yellow star of socialism (removed in 1992 when Mongolia had a new Constitution) is an ideogram called the *syonbo*. This includes a traditional Buddhist yin-yang symbol as well as numerous other elements, whose interpretation yields a cluster of concepts including that of the five elements (earth, air, fire, water, the aether), death to enemies, the value of friendship and others.

POPULATION: 2,100,000
CAPITAL: Ulan Bator (Ulaanbaatar)
AREA: 610,000 sq mi (1,566,500 km²)
LANGUAGES: Mongolian, Kazakh
RELIGIONS: Shamanism, Buddhism, Islam; atheism predominant

MOROCCO
The Kingdom of Morocco

Before 1915 Morocco, like many other Arab countries, flew a plain red flag; the green five-pointed star was added, presumably at the urging of the French, in order to obviate confusion. Initially the flag was for use only on land; it became the true national flag only in 1956, when Morocco regained the independence she had lost in 1912, becoming first a sultanate and then almost at once (1957) a kingdom. This particular pentagram is often called the Seal of Solomon or Solomon's Seal; this term should, in fact, be applied only to a rather similar-looking hexagram, best known outside the field of magic as the Star of David, as depicted on the flag of Israel (*q.v.*).

POPULATION: 24,000,000
CAPITAL: Rabat
AREA: 177,000 sq mi (459,000 km²)
LANGUAGES: Arabic, Berber, French, Spanish
RELIGION: Islam

MOZAMBIQUE
The Republic of Mozambique

The flag adopted by Mozambique on gaining its independence from Portugal in 1975 had the same colours as that of the main party that had spearheaded the fight for liberation, the Frente de Libertaçao de Moçambique (FRELIMO), but a very different design. It was adopted in 1983. The symbols in the red triangle are drawn from the country's coat of arms: the yellow star expresses internationalism, the book education, the hoe agriculture and the Kalashnikov rifle the struggle to attain and if necessary to retain independence. Agriculture and the independence struggle are symbolized also by the use of green and red, respectively, while the white is for peace, the yellow for the nation's mineral resources and the black for the people.

POPULATION: 14,931,000
CAPITAL: Maputo
AREA: 303,000 sq mi (785,000 km²)
LANGUAGES: Portuguese, indigenous languages
RELIGIONS: Animism, Christianity, Islam

NAMIBIA
The Republic of Namibia

Until March 1990 Namibia was a territory technically described as "unlawfully occupied" by South Africa – i.e., its government was enforcedly a puppet of the apartheid state. The resistance to the illegal rule had been led by the South-West Africa People's Organization (SWAPO), and it had been widely expected that the SWAPO flag – a straightforward tricolour of blue, red and green in horizontal bands – would be adopted as the national flag. Instead, however, although the colours were indeed adopted, they were used in a quite different arrangement, and a prominent sun was added to symbolize both the climate and the bright light of a nation at last released from servitude.

POPULATION: 1,750,000
CAPITAL: Windhoek
AREA: 318,300 sq mi (824,300 km²)
LANGUAGES: English, Afrikaans, German, Bantu
RELIGIONS: Christianity, indigenous religions

NAURU
The Republic of Nauru

The flag of Nauru was introduced in 1968 when the country attained her independence, having previously been, since 1947, under the joint trusteeship of Australia, New Zealand and the UK; independent Nauru was admitted to the Commonwealth as a special member. The winner of a design competition, the flag has a 12-pointed star symbolizing Nauru herself, lying in the blue Pacific Ocean one degree south of the yellow Equator. The points of the star are for the 12 original tribes of the island.

The arms of Nauru

POPULATION: 9,000
CENTRE OF GOVERNMENT: Yaren
AREA: 8 sq mi (21 km²)
LANGUAGES: Nauruan, English
RELIGION: Christianity (mainly Protestant)

NEPAL
The Kingdom of Nepal

The most striking feature of the Nepalese flag on first sight is its shape: it is the only national flag not to be rectangular. The origin of this shape is fairly obvious: before the late 19th century two pennants were flown together; these were then joined to make a single entity. The two symbols represent the moon (upper) and sun. Until 1951 and their downfall, the sun represented the Ráná family, which had held prime ministerial office and effective control of the nation, while the moon was for the royal family. The modern form of this centuries-old flag dates only from 1962, when the human faces that had previously adorned both symbols were deleted.

POPULATION: 18,250,000
CAPITAL: Katmandu (Kathmandu)
AREA: 54,360 sq mi (140,790 km^2)
LANGUAGES: Nepali, other indigenous languages
RELIGION: Hinduism (Buddhist and Islamic minorities)

NETHERLANDS
The Kingdom of The Netherlands

The red, white and blue tricolour of The Netherlands flag originated in the flags used by supporters – notably at sea – of William the Silent (1533–84), Prince of Orange, in his campaigns to expel the Spanish. The *Prinsenvlag*, as it came to be known, was accepted as the sole Dutch flag from 1597; but from about 1630 the orange band was frequently rendered in red, and in 1796, the year after the country had been conquered by the French, the orange was prohibited, so that the flag shared the colours of the French tricolour. In 1937 the specified shade of blue was changed, but otherwise the flag has remained unaltered.

POPULATION: 14,760,000
CAPITAL: Amsterdam
SEAT OF GOVERNMENT: The Hague (Den Haag, La Haie, 's-Gravenhage)
AREA: 16,050 sq mi (41,550 km^2)
LANGUAGES: Dutch, Frisian
RELIGION: Christianity

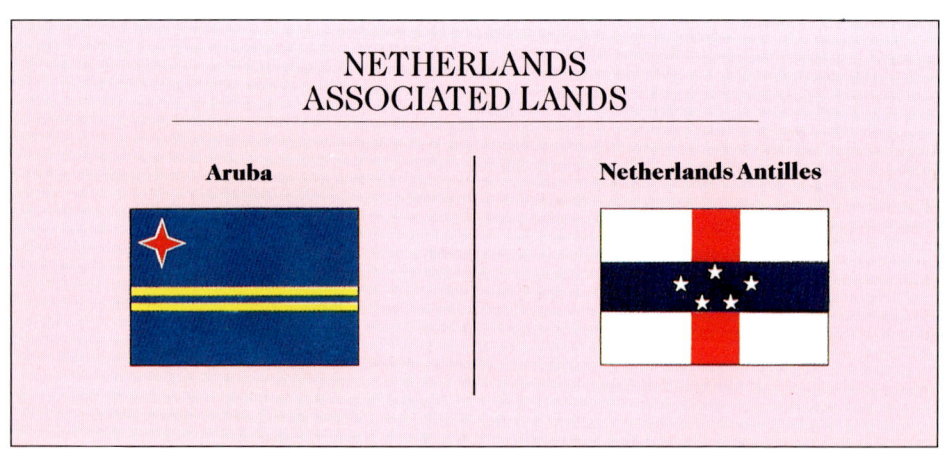

NEW ZEALAND

The flag of New Zealand was designed and introduced for restricted use in 1869 and adopted as the national flag in 1902. It is the British Blue Ensign with a very stylized version of the Southern Cross, showing only four stars; these are red, lined in white. The design has survived New Zealand's becoming a dominion in 1907 and achieving full independence in 1931. A very similar design was introduced in 1870 in Australia (*q.v.*) by the state of Victoria.

The flag of the Queen of New Zealand

POPULATION: 3,300,000
CAPITAL: Wellington
AREA: 103,700 sq mi (268,700 km^2)
LANGUAGES: English, Maori
RELIGION: Christianity (mainly Protestant)

NEW ZEALAND ASSOCIATED LANDS

Niue Island

Tokelau

This territory uses the New Zealand flag.

Cook Islands

NICARAGUA
The Republic of Nicaragua

Until 1821 Nicaragua was part of the captaincy-general of Guatemala, which was ruled by Spain; in that year the captaincy-general declared independence but was almost immediately swallowed up by the Mexican Empire. By 1824 Nicaragua, with Costa Rica, El Salvador, Guatemala and Honduras, had regained their freedom and formed the Central American Federation, an arrangement that was soon to be unravelled, in 1838. The flag of the CAF was a simple blue and white triband, and it was to this design that Nicaragua turned in 1908. The flag may be used plain or with the national arms, which show, in a triangular frame, volcanoes, a rainbow (peace) and the Cap of Liberty. Compare the arms of El Salvador (*q.v.*).

POPULATION: 3,620,000
CAPITAL: Managua
AREA: 50,200 sq mi (130,000 km^2)
LANGUAGE: Spanish
RELIGION: Christianity (almost exclusively RC)

NIGER
The Republic of Niger

The colours of the Niger flag are the same as in that of the Ivory Coast (*q.v.*) and have a similar explanation: orange for the desert land, green for the agricultural land and white for the unity and harmony between their peoples – as well as for the Niger River and its surrounding pastures. The orange disc in the centre of the white stripe is for the sun. Like the Ivory coast, Niger adopted its flag in 1959 and gained independence from France the following year.

POPULATION: 7,250,000
CAPITAL: Niamey
AREA: 490,000 sq mi (1,267,000 km²)
LANGUAGES: French, Hausa
RELIGIONS: Islam, Animism

NIGERIA
The Federal Republic of Nigeria

The Nigerian flag was adopted in 1960 when the country attained its independence from the UK, and was from the winning design of a public competition. The green reflects the importance of the forests and agriculture, while the white represents the desire for peace and unity – a sad irony in the light of the brutal civil war that racked the country between 1967 and 1970, when the Ibo people of Biafra (Iboland), unilaterally declared independence. The war and the concomitant famine cost about a million lives. For the three short years of its existence Biafra had a flag somewhat similar to that of Malawi (*q.v.*), but with the black and red stripes swapped and the rising sun on the black stripe being in gold rather than red.

POPULATION: 105,000,000
CAPITAL: Lagos
AREA: 357,000 sq mi (924,000 km²)
LANGUAGES: English, Yoruba, Hausa, Ibo
RELIGIONS: Islam, Christianity, indigenous religions

NORWAY
The Kingdom of Norway

Norway uses a version of the Scandinavian Cross, seen also in the flags of Denmark (*q.v.*), Finland, Iceland and Sweden (*q.v.*). The Norwegian version dates from 1821, when Norway was still a part of Sweden, having been ceded by Denmark seven years before. The flag is essentially the Danish one but with the addition of a blue cross superimposed on the white, so that the colour scheme expressed Norwegian nationalism.

POPULATION: 4,200,000
CAPITAL: Oslo
AREA: 125,200 sq mi (324,200 km²)
LANGUAGES: Norwegian, Lappish, Finnish
RELIGION: Christianity (mainly Evangelical Lutheran)

OMAN
The Sultanate of Oman

The current flag of Oman was introduced in 1970 (and slightly revised in 1987), replacing the traditional plain red flag. The emblem now used is likewise traditional; it shows a curved dagger fastened over a pair of crossed sabres. The red has retained its customary Islamic significance; the white band is, of course, for peace but also expresses the authority of the imam, while the green band is for Islam and for the Jabel Akhdhar (or Green Mountain range), which lies towards the north of the country.

The emblem of Oman

POPULATION: 1,375,000
CAPITAL: Muscat (Masqat)
AREA: 82,000 sq mi (212,500 km^2)
LANGUAGES: Arabic, English
RELIGION: Islam

PAKISTAN
The Islamic Republic of Pakistan

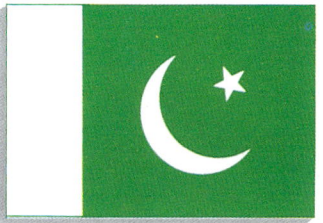

The All-Indian Muslim League, whose activities were largely responsible for Pakistan gaining her independence in 1947, had in 1906 adopted as its flag the Islamic crescent and star on a background of equally Islamic green (in this case described as "tartan" green). It seemed only just that the League's flag be adopted also as the national flag, but at the last moment before independence it was pointed out that, while the majority of the population was Muslim, there were minorities who adhered to other faiths. The vertical white stripe was therefore added to symbolize tolerance of those faiths.

POPULATION: 105,000,000
CAPITAL: Islamabad
AREA: 310,400 sq mi (804,000 km^2)
LANGUAGES: Urdu, English, Punjabi, Sindhi, Pushtu, Baluchi, Bravi
RELIGION: Islam (Hindu and Christian minorities)

PANAMA
The Republic of Panama

Panama achieved its independence (in 1903) from Colombia, of which it had been a province, largely thanks to US assistance. Perhaps in gratitude to their US deliverers, the Panamanians adopted the colours red, white and blue for their flag, although an alternative explanation is that these colours represented the two leading political parties of the time, and that the equal prestige given to each expresses the hope that the two should take turns governing the nation. White has its usual meaning, as do the stars, although the colours of the latter, taken in conjunction with their shape, were intended also to express the rule of law (red) and civic virtues (blue). Since 1979 the flag has been adopted for the canal zone as well.

POPULATION: 2,320,000
CAPITAL: Panama City
AREA: 30,100 sq mi (77,300 km^2)
LANGUAGES: Spanish, English
RELIGION: Christianity (almost exclusively RC)

PAPUA NEW GUINEA
The Independent State of Papua New Guinea

Designed by the winner of a design competition, the flag of Papua New Guinea was adopted in 1971, four years before the attainment of independence from Australia. The Australian presence lingers on in the use of the five-starred version of the Southern Cross, although here the stars are five-pointed. The yellow bird of paradise not only honours a prominent member of the local fauna but also expresses liberty. The colours were selected purely because they are used frequently in the native art.

POPULATION: 3,560,000
CAPITAL: Port Moresby
AREA: 178,000 sq mi (461,700 km^2)
LANGUAGES: English, Pidgin English and perhaps 750 localized languages
RELIGIONS: Christianity, Animism, indigenous religions

PARAGUAY
The Republic of Paraguay

After gaining independence in 1811 Paraguay adopted a tricolour as its flag, but the red-white-blue colour combination was not established until the following year. In 1821 the arms were added to the central white band; they show a golden star, the Star of May, to honour the fact that it was on the night of 14 May that independence was declared. From 1842 a different emblem was used for the reverse side of the flag. This was the so-called Treasury Seal, which depicts a lion guarding the cap of liberty and bears the motto *Paz y Justicia* ("Peace with Justice"). Paraguay's is the only national flag whose reverse differs from its obverse.

POPULATION: 4,040,000
CAPITAL: Asunción
AREA: 157,000 sq mi (407,000 km^2)
LANGUAGES: Spanish, Guarani
RELIGION: Christianity (almost exclusively RC)

PERU
The Republic of Peru

The colours of the Peruvian flag represent peace and justice (white) and the blood of those who lost their lives in the struggle for independence (red). The colour scheme was initially devised in 1820 by the great liberating General José de San Martín (1778–1850) who, it is claimed, was inspired by the sight of a flock of flamingoes flying over his troops. The design suffered alterations until, in 1825, Simón Bolívar (1783–1830) determined that there should be three vertical stripes arranged in the current fashion.

POPULATION: 21,260,000
CAPITAL: Lima
AREA: 496,000 sq mi (1,285,000 km^2)
LANGUAGES: Spanish, Quechua, Aimara
RELIGION: Christianity (almost exclusively RC)

PHILIPPINES
The Republic of the Philippines

The current flag of the Philippines was adopted in 1946, when the country gained independence from the USA. The flag had first been adopted in 1898, the year that the Philippines declared independence from the Spanish, and was almost immediately (and more or less voluntarily) taken over by the USA. The 1898 flag was used until 1907 and from 1921 until the arrival of the Japanese in 1941. The blue is for idealism, the white for purity and peace, and the red for gallantry and determination. The three small yellow stars signify the two main islands plus the Visayan island group; the large star is the sun and has eight rays to commemorate the eight provinces that first took up the torch of independence in 1896.

POPULATION: 58,720,000
CAPITAL: Manila
AREA: 115,800 sq mi (300,000 km^2)
LANGUAGES: Philipino, English, Spanish
RELIGION: Christianity (Islamic minority)

POLAND
The Republic of Poland

The arms of Poland, depicting a white eagle on a red background, date back at least as far as the 13th century, and white and red were adopted as the Polish national colours in 1831. The flag using them, dates from 1919, and since then various revised interpretations have been foisted on to the colours; for example, until the Solidarity movement took over the reins of power in 1989 it was popular to explain the colours as an expression of the people's joint desire for peace and socialism.

POPULATION: 37,900,000
CAPITAL: Warsaw (Warszawa)
AREA: 121,900 sq mi (313,000 km^2)
LANGUAGE: Polish
RELIGION: Christianity (almost exclusively RC)

PORTUGAL
The Portuguese Republic

In 1910 the Portuguese monarchy was ousted and a republic established, and it is from this year that the current flag and the prominence on it of revolutionary red both date. The green, often taken to express hope or the sea, can be traced back to the time of Henry the Navigator (1394–1460), who inspired and sponsored a whole generation of Portuguese maritime explorers. The depiction of the armillary sphere at the centre of the flag likewise links with Henry the Navigator, being an emblem chosen to commemorate the deeds of Henry and his protégés by King Manuel I (1469–1521), whose reign saw a further great surge of Portuguese exploration.

POPULATION: 10,400,000
CAPITAL: Lisbon (Lisboa)
AREA: 35,800 sq mi (92,000 km^2)
LANGUAGE: Portuguese
RELIGION: Christianity (almost exclusively RC)

PORTUGAL – ASSOCIATED LANDS

Azores

Macao
The flag used in Macao is that of Portugal.

Madeira

PUERTO RICO
The Commonwealth of Puerto Rico

Puerto Rico became a commonwealth of the USA in 1952, at which time she adopted as her national flag (which may be flown only in conjunction with the US flag) a design that had first been created in 1895 by the Cuban Revolutionary Party's Puerto Rican branch, an important liberation movement in the struggle for independence from Spain. The flag is very similar to that of Cuba (*q.v.*) but with the stripes in blue and the triangle in red, rather than the other way about. In light of the later history of the two countries' relationships with the USA the similarity is ironic.

POPULATION: 3,600,000
CAPITAL: San Juan
AREA: 3,450 sq mi (8,900 km^2)
LANGUAGES: Spanish, English
RELIGION: Christianity (mainly RC)

QATAR
The State of Qatar

Before 1820 a number of the states around the Persian Gulf had the plain red flags of the Kharidjite sect of Islam. Many vessels flying such flags practised piracy on occidental ships, and so in that year the British decreed that in future all such vessels would be assumed to be pirates unless their flags bore white in addition to the red. It was not until the mid-1850s that Qatar complied with this dictum. Her flag was then very similar to that of Bahrain (*q.v.*), but in 1949 the problem was solved by Qatar replacing the red by a curious deep maroon. This may have been a matter of official recognition following long after the fact, since the red vegetable dyes used to colour the flag may well have faded to a shade like this in the heat of the desert sun.

POPULATION: 370,000
CAPITAL: Doha (Ad Dawhah)
AREA: 4,400 sq mi (11,450 km^2)
LANGUAGES: Arabic, English
RELIGION: Islam

ROMANIA

Until the downfall of the repressive communist regime of Nicolae Ceauşescu (1918–89) in 1989 the Romanian flag bore communist arms in its central yellow stripe. Before 1859 the land that is now Romania consisted of two separate principalities, Wallachia and Moldavia. The Wallachian colours were blue and yellow; those of Moldavia were blue and red. When the two were united it was simple to devise a flag representing all three of the relevant colours, and this was done as early as 1848, when nationalist rumblings were beginning to stir the land. The flag was accepted in 1859 when the two principalities united (two years later they jointly took the name Romania), and in 1866 a rearrangement to make the flag resemble the French tricolour was adopted; this is the form in use today.

POPULATION: 23,050,000
CAPITAL: Bucharest (Bucuresti)
AREA: 92,000 sq mi (237,500 km^2)
LANGUAGE: Romanian
RELIGION: Christianity (mainly Romanian Orthodox)

RUSSIA
The Russian Federation

The Russian Federation is a loosely knit collection of republics including much of what was until 1991 the Union of Soviet Socialist Republics; many of the other SSRs have become unitary states and now have equal ranking with it in the Commonwealth of Independent States, of which it is the largest member. There are 17 autonomous republics within the Federation; namely Bashkir, Buryat, Chechen-Ingust, Chuvash, Dagestan, Kabardino-Balkar, Kalmyk, Kara-Kalpak, Karelia, Korni, Mari, Mordovia, North Ossetia, Tatar, Tuva, Udmurt and Yakut.

POPULATION: 143,078,000
CAPITAL: Moscow (Moskva)
AREA: 6,592,800 sq mi (17,075,400 km^2)
LANGUAGES: Russian and numerous others
RELIGIONS: Christianity, Islam (Jewish minority)

RWANDA
The Republic of Rwanda

In January 1961 the Hutu people of the northern part of the Belgian-administered UN Trust Territory of Ruanda-Urundi – the southern part is now Burundi (*q.v.*) – overthrew the ruling Tutsi people and declared their country an independent republic; recognized by Belgium in the following year. The first flag raised in 1961, a tricolour in the Pan-African colours of red, green and yellow, was much like that of Mali (*q.v.*), and the similarity became an identity a few weeks later when Mali modified her flag. The Hutu therefore changed their flag which unfortunately made it identical with that of Guinea, and so a prominent R – standing for Rwanda, referendum and revolution was added to the central stripe to avoid confusion.

POPULATION: 6,755,000
CAPITAL: Kigali
AREA: 10,200 sq mi (26,300 km^2)
LANGUAGES: Kinyarwanda, French, Kiswahili
RELIGIONS: Christianity, indigenous religions, Islam

ST KITTS AND NEVIS
The Federation of Saint Kitts and Nevis

Independence came to St Kitts-Nevis in 1983, and with it the current flag; until 1980 the country had been, with Anguilla (*q.v.*), part of the associate state of St Kitts-Nevis-Anguilla. The colours are green for fertility, red for the liberation struggle, black for the African heritage and yellow for sunshine; the white stars express hope and freedom.

POPULATION: 49,000
CAPITAL: Basseterre
AREA: 100 sq mi (260 km^2)
LANGUAGE: English
RELIGION: Christianity (mainly Protestant)

ST LUCIA

The basic design of the St Lucia flag was established in 1967, when the country became internally self-governing; it was created by a local artist. In 1979 St Lucia attained full independence, and the flag's proportions were amended and the central symbol enlarged. That symbol represents the Pitons, twin conical volcanic plugs that rise sheerly and impressively from the sea at the southwest of the island. The black and white of the major triangle are for the black and white communities and the harmony between them; the yellow triangle is for sandy beaches; and the blue background is for the ocean.

POPULATION: 146,600
CAPITAL: Castries
AREA: 240 sq mi (620 km^2)
LANGUAGES: English, French
RELIGION: Christianity (mainly RC)

ST VINCENT
Saint Vincent and the Grenadines

St Vincent and the Grenadines became internally self-governing in 1969 and attained full independence in 1979, at which time it adopted the predecessor of its current flag. In 1792 Captain William Bligh (*c*1753–1815), brought to St Vincent from Tahiti some breadfruit trees with which he hoped to provide a food-source for the slaves. The slaves preferred the plentiful indigenous foods, but Bligh's effort is still acknowledged in the nation's flag. The 1979 flag had, on its central yellow stripe, the national arms supported on a breadfruit leaf. In 1985, the arms disappeared, and the leaf was represented by three green diamonds. The yellow stripe was broadened, and the thin white stripes that had separated it from the blue and green were eliminated.

POPULATION: 114,000
CAPITAL: Kingstown
AREA: 150 sq mi (390 km^2)
LANGUAGES: English, French
RELIGION: Christianity (mainly Protestant)

SAN MARINO
The Republic of San Marino

San Marino has the curious distinction of being the world's smallest republic. Its flag is known from as far back as 1797. The colours are taken from the arms: the white represents the snow on Monte Titano and the clouds in the sky above it, and the blue signifies the sky itself.

POPULATION: 23,000
CAPITAL: San Marino
AREA: 24 sq mi (61 km^2)
LANGUAGE: Italian
RELIGION: Christianity (almost exclusively RC)

SÃO TOMÉ AND PRÍNCIPE
The Democratic Republic of São Tomé and Príncipe

The two black stars in the flag, adopted in 1975 on the attainment of independence from Portugal, represent the republic's two islands. The colours are in accordance with the Pan-African colours and have their customary meanings except for the yellow, which is taken to represent the nation's cocoa plantations. The flag is closely based on that adopted three years earlier by the MLSTP (Movement for the Liberation of São Tomé and Príncipe), the sole difference being that the yellow stripe is wider in the national flag.

The arms of São Tomé

POPULATION: 115,000
CAPITAL: São Tomé
AREA: 372 sq mi (965 km^2)
LANGUAGES: Portuguese, Creole, indigenous languages
RELIGIONS: Christianity, Animism

SAUDI ARABIA
The Kingdom of Saudi Arabia

From about the mid-18th century the Saud family strove to dominate the many warring peoples of the Arabian peninsula, and they took as their flag the green banner believed to have been used by Muhammad himself; by 1932 they had established the Kingdom of Saudi Arabia. The text in Arabic was added to the flag in 1901; it is a statement analogous to the Christian Creed, and reads: "There is no God but Allah, and Muhammad is Allah's Prophet." The emblem of the sword, incorporated in 1906, refers specifically to Ibn Saud (1880–1953), who, after much conquest, became Saudi Arabia's first king and, more generally, to the military triumphs of Islam.

POPULATION: 14,000,000
CAPITAL: Riyadh (Ar-Riyad)
AREA: 830,000 sq mi (2,150,000 km^2)
LANGUAGES: Arabic, English
RELIGION: Islam

POPULATION: 7,000,000
CAPITAL: Dakar
AREA: 76,000 sq mi (196,700 km^2)
LANGUAGES: French, Wolof and other indigenous languages
RELIGION: Islam (Christian and traditionalist minorities)

SENEGAL
The Republic of Senegal

In 1960 Mali (*q.v.*) and Senegal became independent together, having in the previous year federated – to form the Federation of Mali – and adopted a joint flag; shortly after independence the two nations agreed to go their separate ways, Mali keeping both name and flag. Senegal altered the flag simply by substituting a five-pointed green star for the central figure of the 1959 flag. The star expresses unity, peace, hope and socialism.

The arms of Senegal

POPULATION: 67,000
CAPITAL: Victoria
AREA: 175 sq mi (455 km^2)
LANGUAGES: Creole, French, English
RELIGION: Christianity (mainly RC)

SEYCHELLES
The Republic of Seychelles

On attaining independence in 1976 the Seychelles adopted a flag that combined the colours of the two leading political parties, the Democrats and the Seychelles People's United Party, led by Albert René (1935–), who became the country's first prime minister and who, in 1977, ousted Mancham (the Democratic leader and first national president). SPUP changed the flag immediately on entering office, substituting a design very similar to that of its own flag except for the omission of stylized rising sun of liberty. The meanings of the colours are said to be white for the waves and the resources of the Indian Ocean, green for agriculture and vegetation, and red for the customary mixture of blood, sweat, tears and revolutionary fervour.

POPULATION: 4,000,000
CAPITAL: Freetown
AREA: 28,000 sq mi (72,000 km^2)
LANGUAGES: English, Krio, Mende, Temne
RELIGIONS: Animism, Islam, Christianity

SIERRA LEONE
The Republic of Sierra Leone

The flag of Sierra Leone was adopted in 1961 when the country attained its independence from the UK. Blue is for the Atlantic, green for agriculture and white for peace, justice, virtue, unity and all the similar sentiments. The country's name, which means "lion mountain", was given to it by the Portuguese sailors who discovered the country in 1462, probably because one of the mountains on Cape Sierra Leone (the peninsula on which Freetown stands) can be perceived to resemble a crouching lion; a more fanciful explanation is that they mistook distant thunder for the roaring of giant lions. Whichever, lions feature prominently in the country's arms.

SINGAPORE
The Republic of Singapore

The Singapore flag, in the traditional Malaysian colours of red and white, was adopted in 1959 when the country attained self-government as a UK colony. Since then it has survived a period as part of the Federation of Malaysia, between 1963 and the country's secession in 1965, in which latter year Singapore gained full independence. The white is as ever for virtue and purity and the red for the universal fellowship of mankind. The crescent expresses the youth of the state, and the five five-pointed stars represent the five ideals through adherence to which the state hopes to make its future: democracy, peace, progress, justice and equality.

POPULATION: 2,670,000
CAPITAL: Singapore
AREA: 240 sq mi (620 km²)
LANGUAGES: Malaysian, Chinese, English, Tamil
RELIGIONS: Buddhism, Islam, Taoism, Hinduism, Christianity, Confucianism

SLOVAKIA
The Slovak Republic

Slovakia became an independent state in January 1993; formerly part of Czechoslovakia. Czechoslovakia was formed in 1918, after the collapse of the Austro-Hungarian Empire out of the Austrian possessions Bohemia, Moravia and part of Silesia as well as out of former Hungarian possessions Slovakia and Ruthenia (the latter added in 1920). World War II effected further changes; in 1948 communism triumphed, and in 1969 the federation of two separate republics, Slovakia and The Czech Socialist Republic, was established as the Czechoslovak Socialist Republic. Slovakia's flag has a tricolour in the traditional Slavonic colours of white, blue and red. To differentiate from the Russian flag, it has added a crest, which dates back more than 1000 years.

POPULATION: 5,274,335
CAPITAL: Bratislava
AREA: 18,924 sq mi (49,014 km²)
LANGUAGES: Slovak, Hungarian, Czech
RELIGIONS: Christian (RC), Evangelic, Greek Catholic

SLOVENIA
The Republic of Slovenia

Until 1918, when Yugoslavia (*q.v.*) was manufactured as the Kingdom of the Serbs, Croats and Slovenes, Slovenia was a province of Austria and called Carniola. It has been a unitary state since 1991, when it seceded from Yugoslavia after a short period of civil war which was less bloody than that suffered by Croatia (*q.v.*) – largely because Croatia acted as a buffer between Slovenia and the dominant Serbia. The colours of the flag are Slav.

POPULATION: 1,891,864
CAPITAL: Ljubljana
AREA: 7,817 sq mi (20,250 km²)
LANGUAGE: Slovene (a Romanized variety of Serbo-Croat)
RELIGION: Roman Catholicism

SOLOMON ISLANDS

The result of official discussion and a design competition, the flag of the Solomon Islands was created in 1977 and adopted the following year. The five five-pointed stars on a background of blue represent the archipelagian nation's five administrative units surrounded by the Pacific (and not, as is sometimes claimed, its main islands, for of these there are six). The green is for vegetal lushness and the yellow for sunshine.

POPULATION: 300,000
CAPITAL: Honiara
AREA: 11,500 sq mi (29,800 km²)
LANGUAGES: English, Pidgin English, indigenous languages
RELIGIONS: Christianity, indigenous religions

The arms of the Solomon Islands

SOMALIA
The Somali Democratic Republic

Adopted in 1950 by Italian Somaliland, then a UN Trust Territory, the flag was adopted in 1960 by the new country of Somalia, which was formed out of the Italian and British Somalilands. It is based on the United Nations flag, with which it shares its colours (although in the case of Somalia the blue is sometimes claimed to represent the bright sky). The star expresses the cause of African freedom, and its five points represent the five divisions into which history, geography and politics had sundered the Somali peoples: these five divisions were, in territorial terms, the Somalis of French Somaliland (now Djibouti, *q.v.*), British and Italian Somaliland, northern Kenya and Ethiopia.

POPULATION: 7,110,000
CAPITAL: Mogadishu (Mogadiscio, Muqdisho)
AREA: 246,300 sq mi (638,000 km²)
LANGUAGE: Somali
RELIGION: Islam

SOUTH AFRICA
The Republic of South Africa

South Africa's current flag was introduced in 1928, and until 1957 it was always flown in conjunction with the Union Jack. It has the red-white-blue of the flag of the Netherlands, to which country many of the minority white population owe their ancestry. On the central stripe is superimposed an emblem made up out of the Union Jack and the flags of the Transvaal and the Orange Free State; the UK flag represents the two British colonies (Natal and Cape Province). The aim was to placate those of British and those of Dutch descent; in this it was something of a failure – and it is staggering that no one seems to have paid heed to the far more serious looming problem of the relationship between the whites in general and the vast black majority of the nation's people.

POPULATION: 33,750,000
CAPITAL: Pretoria
AREA: 470,000 sq mi (1,220,000 km²)
LANGUAGES: Afrikaans, English, Bantu
RELIGIONS: Christianity, indigenous religions (Hindu, Islam and Jewish)

SPAIN
The Kingdom of Spain

If tradition is to be believed, the colours of Spain date back to the 9th century, when the French King Charles I the Bald (823–77) granted colours to the Count of Aragon by smearing his blood-stained hands on the latter's plain leather shield. Whatever the truth, certainly red and white stripes were the recognized sign of Aragon by the 12th century, and in 1795, with the arms of León and Castile, they were used in the national flag. At the start of the Second Republic, in 1931, the purple, included in the flag from 1873–5, was again deployed, however, only a few years later, in 1936, the dictator Francisco Franco intervened to restore the old design except with, now, a new coat of arms. In 1981, six years after his death, this was dropped.

POPULATION: 39,100,000
CAPITAL: Madrid
AREA: 195,000 sq mi (505,000 km^2)
LANGUAGES: Castilian, Catalan, Galician, Basque
RELIGION: Christianity (almost exclusively RC)

SRI LANKA
The Democratic Socialist Republic of Sri Lanka

The symbol of the lion clutching a sword was adopted for the national flag when the country gained independence, as Ceylon, from the UK in 1948; with four attendant stylized pagodas, it had served as the flags of the kings of Kandy since ancient times. In 1951 the two vertical stripes were added to the flag to acknowledge the country's minority groups: orange for the Tamils (Hindus) and green for the Muslims. In 1972, when the country changed its name and declared itself a republic, the pagodas were replaced with stylized leaves from the sacred bo tree under which the Buddha meditated, and in 1978 the design of these leaves was modified towards greater realism.

POPULATION: 16,000,000
CAPITAL: Colombo
AREA: 25,300 sq mi (65,600 km^2)
LANGUAGES: Sinhala, Tamil, English
RELIGIOUS: Buddhism, Hinduism (Islamic and Christian minorities)

SUDAN
The Republic of Sudan

Like that of Jordan (*q.v.*) and others, the Sudanese flag is in the Pan-Arab colours of red, white, green and black. From 1899 until 1956 Sudan was an Anglo-Egyptian condominium. Independence brought with it a green, yellow and blue tricolour, which survived a military coup in 1958 and the restoration of civilian rule in 1964, but not the military coup of 1969, which brought to power the regime of the dictatorial President Jaafar Nimeiri (1929–), which held a design competition to determine a new flag; the winning design was adopted in 1970.

POPULATION: 23,800,000
CAPITAL: Khartoum
AREA: 965,000 sq mi (2,500,000 km^2)
LANGUAGES: Arabic, English, Nubian
RELIGIONS: Islam, indigenous religions (Christian minority)

SURINAM
The Republic of Surinam

POPULATION: 415,000
CAPITAL: Paramaribo
AREA: 63,000 sq mi (163,250 km^2)
LANGUAGES: Dutch, English, Hindi, Javanese, Chinese, "Surinamese"
RELIGIONS: Christianity, Hinduism, Islam

Surinam was English from 1650 until 1667, when it was ceded to the Netherlands in exchange for what was then New Amsterdam – now known as New York. Despite occasional British occupations, the country was named Dutch Guiana until 1948; in 1954 it became internally self-governing, and finally in 1975 it became an independent republic, with a new flag which has remained unchanged since then. The dominant colours, red, green and white, represent the three main political groupings as well as having subsidiary meanings (red for progress, green for agriculture, white for purity). The star has five points for the nation's five ethnic communities and is yellow as an expression of the golden future.

SWAZILAND
The Kingdom of Swaziland

POPULATION: 740,000
CAPITAL: Mbabane
AREA: 6,700 sq mi (17,400 km^2)
LANGUAGES: English, Swazi
RELIGIONS: Christianity, indigenous religions

The Swaziland flag has a design very similar to one first given in 1941 to the Emasotsha regiment of the Swazi Pioneer Corps during the time the land was still British; it was adopted, virtually unchanged, when Swaziland became independent in 1968. The blue is for peace, the yellow for mineral resources and the red for battle. The shield is of oxhide and bears a tassel of royalty; the fighting staff beneath the two spears bears two of these tassels, which denote royalty.

The arms of Swaziland

SWEDEN
The Kingdom of Sweden

POPULATION: 8,450,000
CAPITAL: Stockholm
AREA: 174,000 sq mi (450,000 km^2)
LANGUAGE: Swedish
RELIGION: Christianity (almost exclusively Evangelical Lutheran)

Sweden uses a version of the Scandinavian Cross. Although officially adopted only in 1906, the Swedish version of this basic design has a very long history. It seems to have been adopted about 1520 as the flag under which the Swedish nationalists fought against their Danish oppressors. The colours came originally from the use in the national arms of three golden crowns on a blue background.

SWITZERLAND
The Swiss Confederation

The Swiss flag is the only national flag to be square. In its current form it was adopted only in 1848 (revised in 1889), but it is of much greater antiquity than that. A form of it seems to have been in use in the canton of Schwyz by the end of the 13th century; in 1339 the federated cantons of Schwyz, Lucerne, Nidwalden and Uri adopted it as their common flag in their struggle for liberation from the Holy Roman Empire. The flag survived Switzerland's full independence in 1648, occupation by the French in 1798–1815, and ensuing religious strife that threatened to split the country; it has become a symbol for neutrality.

POPULATION: 6,570,000
CAPITAL: Berne (Bern)
AREA: 15,950 sq mi (41,300 km²)
LANGUAGES: German, French, Italian, Romansch
RELIGION: Christianity

SYRIA
The Syrian Arab Republic

The flag of Syria is in the Pan-Arab colours, like that of Jordan (*q.v.*) and others. When Egypt (*q.v.*) and Syria (and later North Yemen) formed the United Arab Republic in 1958, all three shared very similar flags, the Syrian version having two green stars on the central band of a red-white-green arrangement. In 1963 it adopted a red-white-black arrangement with three green stars in the central band, thereby sharing the same flag as Iraq (*q.v.*), in the unfulfilled expectation that Egypt, Syria and Iraq would soon come together. When Libya, Egypt and Syria formed the short-lived Federation of Arab Republics in 1971, Syria replaced the three stars with a golden hawk. This was subsequently replaced with two green stars.

POPULATION: 11,400,000
CAPITAL: Damascus (Dimashq)
AREA: 71,500 sq mi (185,200 km²)
LANGUAGE: Arabic
RELIGION: Islam (Christian minority)

TAJIKISTAN
The Republic of Tajikistan

Tajikistan has been a unitary state since 1991, having become so at the time of the general dissolution of the Union of Soviet Socialist Republics. The land is extremely mountainous; it contains the peak which was, before the collapse of the union, the highest in the USSR, Communism Peak, in the Pamir Range. Tajikistan's history is one of foreign domination – Alexander the Great was one of many to count it among his occupations. During the 16th century it was taken over by Bukhara (Bokhara), a powerful kingdom centred on what is now the Bukhara region of Uzbekistan (*q.v.*) and which was ceded to Russia in 1868. The object at the centre of the new flag is a crown, surmounted by an arc of seven stars; this emblem also forms the crest of the national arms.

POPULATION: 4,500,000
CAPITAL: Dushanbe
AREA: 55,250 sq mi (143,100 km²)
LANGUAGES: Tadzhik, Russian
RELIGION: Islam

TAIWAN
The Republic of China*

The flag of Taiwan is that adopted by the Guomindang government of Chiang Kai-shek (1887–1975) for China as a whole in 1928 and used as the national flag until the communist victory in the Chinese Civil War in 1949 and the subsequent Guomindang flight to the island of Taiwan; earlier the flag had been used by the Guomindang under Sun Yat-sen (1866–1925). The red is for the nation of China – just as it is in the flag of the People's Republic – and the small rectangle shows, against a blue sky, a white sun (representing the yang principle) whose 12 points stand for the hours of the day and of the night.

*This is a self-styled title, not recognised internationally.

POPULATION: 19,700,000
CAPITAL: T'ai-pei
AREA: 13,800 sq mi (35,975 km^2)
LANGUAGES: Mandarin, Hakka, Hokkien
RELIGIONS: Buddhism, Taoism, Christianity; also Confucianism

TANZANIA
The United Republic of Tanzania

Adopted in 1964 when Tanganyika united with Zanzibar to become Tanzania, the flag combines elements from those adopted by the two countries on attainment of their individual independences, Tanganyika in 1961 and Zanzibar in 1963. The colours of the leading Tanganyikan political party were green and black – the flag had also thin yellow stripes – and those of its counterpart in Zanzibar were blue, black and green. The yellow stripes survived in the new flag, which otherwise included the colours of both parties in bands set diagonally to forestall any questions of ranking. The meanings of the colours are said to be green for agriculture, black for the people and blue for the sea, with the yellow veins referring to the nation's mineral resources.

POPULATION: 24,000,000
CAPITAL: Dar es Salaam
AREA: 365,000 sq mi (945,000 km^2)
LANGUAGES: Swahili, English
RELIGIONS: Christianity, Islam, indigenous religions (Hindu minority)

THAILAND
The Kingdom of Thailand

During the 19th century the Thai flag featured a white elephant, one of the symbols of both the country itself ("The Land of the White Elephant") and its monarchs ("The Kings of the White Elephant"). In the latter part of the century the flag was plain red with a central white elephant; in 1916 horizontal white stripes above and below the beast were introduced; and in 1917 the animal was omitted altogether. Later that year, as a gesture of solidarity with the Allies in World War I, a central blue band was inserted so that the colours matched those of the French flag.

POPULATION: 54,550,000
CAPITAL: Bangkok (Krung Thep)
AREA: 200,000 sq mi (515,000 km^2)
LANGUAGE: Thai
RELIGION: Buddhism (Islamic minority)

The emblem of Thailand

TOGO
The Republic of Togo

Introduced in 1960 when the country gained its independence, the flag of Togo, which is in the Pan-African colours, seems to have been inspired to some measure by the Stars and Stripes or by one of its imitators. The five stripes represent the republic's five major administrative units; the white star is for purity, unity and the bright inspiration of progress; yellow is for mineral reserves; green for agriculture and vegetal abundance; and red is for bloodshed, patriotic fervour and fidelity.

POPULATION: 3,250,000
CAPITAL: Lomé
AREA: 22,000 sq mi (56,750 km^2)
LANGUAGES: French, Ewe, Kabra, indigenous languages
RELIGIONS: indigenous religions, Christianity, Islam

TONGA
The Kingdom of Tonga

The design of the flag of Tonga was established as inalterable in the first national constitution in 1875 at the express behest of King Taufa'ahau Tupou George I (1797–1893), who wished the flag to reflect his own – and, he hoped, his subjects' – devotion to Christianity; in fact, the flag was in use for about a decade before its constitutional adoption. Because of the monarch's keystone role in the nation's history, there has been no move to amend this aspect of the constitution; the red cross itself has become Tonga's national emblem. The flag has further Christian symbolism in that its red is for the blood of Christ shed on the cross.

POPULATION: 116,000
CAPITAL: Nuku'alofa
AREA: 290 sq mi (750 km^2)
LANGUAGES: Tongan, English
RELIGION: Christianity (mainly Protestant)

TRINIDAD AND TOBAGO
The Republic of Trinidad and Tobago

The flag of Trinidad and Tobago was adopted in 1962 when the country gained its independence and survived unchanged when the nation became a republic in 1976. The design has no obvious symbolism (it was determined by a committee). The colours were selected for various reasons: black is for the islands' wealth, for their inhabitants' fortitude and for those inhabitants themselves; red is for the warmth and vitality of the sun, the people and the nation; and white is for purity, emancipation and the waves breaking on the nation's shores.

POPULATION: 1,245,000
CAPITAL: Port of Spain
AREA: 1,980 sq mi (5130 km^2)
LANGUAGES: English, Hindi, French, Spanish
RELIGIONS: Christianity, Hinduism, (Islamic minority)

TUNISIA
The Tunisian Republic

The flag of Turkey (*q.v.*) was in widespread use in Tunisia from about the beginning of the 19th century, and in 1835 a version of it was introduced that has survived more or less unchanged until today. On Tunisia's attainment of independence from the French the flag became the national flag. The symbolism is as for the Turkish flag except for the inclusion of a white circle representing the sun.

POPULATION: 7,810,000
CAPITAL: Tunis
AREA: 63,200 sq mi (163,700 km^2)
LANGUAGES: Arabic, French
RELIGION: Islam (Jewish and Christian minorities)

The arms of Tunisia

TURKEY
The Republic of Turkey

The crescent moon and the star are ancient symbols – and red a colour – of both Islam and, more specifically, of Turkey and the Ottoman Empire. Ottoman flags bearing the crescent symbol are known from as early as the 16th century, and in 1793 the crescent and star appeared for the first time together on the Turkish flag – although the star had six rather than the now more customary five points. For a short period in the early 1920s the flag was Islamic green, but on the declaration of the republic under Kemal Atatürk (1881–1938) it reverted to red.

POPULATION: 52,420,000
CAPITAL: Ankara
AREA: 301,400 sq mi (780,500 km^2)
LANGUAGES: Turkish, Arabic, Greek, Circassian, Armenian, Yiddish, Kurdish
RELIGION: Islam

TURKMENISTAN

Turkmenistan has been a unitary state since 1991, having become so at the time of the general dissolution of the Union of Soviet Socialist Republics. Of the land, about 90 per cent is desert, notably the vast Kara Kum Desert (area about 118,500 sq mi/ 300,000 km^2). For some reason, numerous outside powers have chosen over the centuries to invade Turkmenistan; the modern republic was established within the USSR in 1925. Turkmenistan's flag is unusual in having a carpet-like pattern in the hoist comprising five traditional elements in black, white and orange on a "claret" coloured background. The main part of the flag has an Islamic green background and contains a crescent and five stars. The flag was adopted in 1992.

POPULATION: 3,200,000
CAPITAL: Aschabad (Ashkhabad)
AREA: 188,455 sq mi (488,100 km^2)
LANGUAGES: Turkoman (one of the Turkic group), Russian
RELIGION: Islam

TUVALU

As the Ellice Islands, Tuvalu was until 1975 part of the UK colony of the Gilbert and Ellice Islands; in that year it was separated from the Gilberts (now Kiribati, *q.v.*) as Tuvalu, and in 1978 it became an independent state and adopted a new flag based on a competition-winning design. The UK past is very evident, for this is essentially the Blue Ensign but done in a very pale blue (as in the flag of Fiji, *q.v.*). The nine golden stars represent the state's nine major islands, and their disposition is the same as that of the islands in the ocean (but with west at the top of the flag).

POPULATION: 9,700
CAPITAL: Funafuti (Vaiaku)
AREA: 10 sq mi (26 km^2)
LANGUAGES: Tuvaluan, English
RELIGION: Christianity (mainly Protestant)

UGANDA
The Republic of Uganda

Just before Uganda gained its independence in 1962, the Democratic Party unexpectedly lost power to the Uganda People's Congress Party led by Milton Obote (1925–   ), who duly became the country's first prime minister. Unfortunately, a new national flag had already been prepared in the colours of the Democratic Party, and so some rapid work had to be done to create a revised version, in the UPC colours of black (for the people and for Africa), yellow (for the sun) and red (for universal fraternity), in time for the great occasion. The badge in the centre shows a crested crane on a white disc, a long-standing emblem of the country.

POPULATION: 17,200,000
CAPITAL: Kampala
AREA: 91,100 sq mi (236,000 km^2)
LANGUAGES: English, Swahili, Bantu, Luganda
RELIGIONS: Christianity, Islam

UKRAINE

Ukraine has been a unitary state since 1991, having become so at the time of the general dissolution of the Union of Soviet Socialist Republics. It was the third largest of the republics of the old USSR and second only to the Russian Federation (*q.v.*) in terms of population, industrial production and agricultural output. Ukraine's flag dates back to 1848 and was used for the independent state formed after the fall of the Russian Empire. Independence lasted only until 1921, when it became part of the USSR; the flag was thereafter only used in exile until the country became once more independent in 1991. The colours are taken from the arms of Galicia, blue with a golden lion, but are often described as the blue sky over the waving corn of the steppes.

POPULATION: 51,704,000
CAPITAL: Kiev
AREA: 233,000 sq mi (603,700 km^2)
LANGUAGES: Ukrainian, Russian
RELIGION: Christianity

UNITED ARAB EMIRATES

Like the flag of Jordan (*q.v.*) and others, that of the United Arab Emirates is in the Pan-Arab colours. The sheikdoms that came together in 1971 in this federation – Abu Dhabi, Ajman, Dubai, Fujairah, Ras al-Khaimah (joined 1972), Sharjah and Umm al-Qaiwain – had all (except Fujairah) been among those Gulf states that, in 1820, signed an agreement with the British to add white to their traditional plain red flags of the Kharidjite sect of Islam, to distinguish their vessels from pirate ones; from 1892 they were UK protectorates as the Trucial States. On independence they chose the Pan-Arab colours but with the red band placed vertically as a reminder of their Kharidjite flag.

POPULATION: 1,500,000
CAPITAL: Abu Dhabi (Abu Zaby)
AREA: 32,630 sq mi (83,660 km²)
LANGUAGES: Arabic, English
RELIGION: Islam

UNITED KINGDOM OF GREAT BRITAIN AND NORTHERN IRELAND

POPULATION: 57,100,000
CAPITAL: London
AREA: 94,250 sq mi (244,100 km²)
LANGUAGES: English, Gaelic, Welsh, Cornish, Erse
RELIGION: Christianity (mainly Protestant) (Islamic, Jewish, Hindu and Sikh minorities)

The national flag of the United Kingdom is the Union Flag, more commonly known as the Union Jack and, along with the Stars and Stripes and the French tricolour, it is one of the best known flags in the world. It was adopted in 1801 and has remained unchanged. It is made up from the crosses of St George (England) and St Andrew (Scotland) and a cross, generally called St Patrick's Cross, of the powerful Geraldine family of Ireland. The earliest form of the flag was introduced in 1606, three years after James VI of Scotland (1566–1625) had succeeded Elizabeth I of England (1533–1603) to become King James I of Scotland and England. It was formed by superimposing the Cross of St George on the Cross of St Andrew, using the latter's blue background also for the flag as a whole except for a thin white edging of the St George's Cross, red on blue being a heraldic taboo. During the Commonwealth, from 1649, Oliver Cromwell (1599–1658) superimposed the image of a gaelic harp, but this was dropped on the Restoration of the Monarchy

UK COUNTRIES

England

Scotland

Wales

Northern Ireland

in 1660. In 1707 came the Act of Union, the legislative incorporation of England and Scotland, and Queen Anne (1665–1714) approved the original flag for use in all flags, standards, ensigns and banners. 1800 saw the union with Ireland, and when this came into effect in 1801, the new version of the Union Jack was adopted. This integrates the arms of the red Cross of St Patrick with those of the white Cross of St Andrew in such a way that neither is seen to be superior to the other, the red stripes being placed above the white stripes in the right-hand quarters and below them in the left-hand quarters. The modern flag is authorized for use only on land and by land forces. At sea it may be flown only by a craft bearing the monarch or by the flagship of a fleet commanded by an admiral. For all other uses at sea the design must be incorporated as the top left-hand corner of a plain red or blue or white flag – called, respectively, the Red Ensign (for merchant ships) and the Blue Ensign (for the Royal Naval Reserve) – or on a Cross of St George – the White Ensign (used by warships and, from 1864, reserved exclusively for the Royal Navy). The ensign used by the Royal Air Force has a pale blue background and incorporates the RAF emblem of a red, white and blue target. Adaptations of the ensigns have been adopted by various Commonwealth countries and UK dependencies and territories, by some Canadian and all the Australian states.

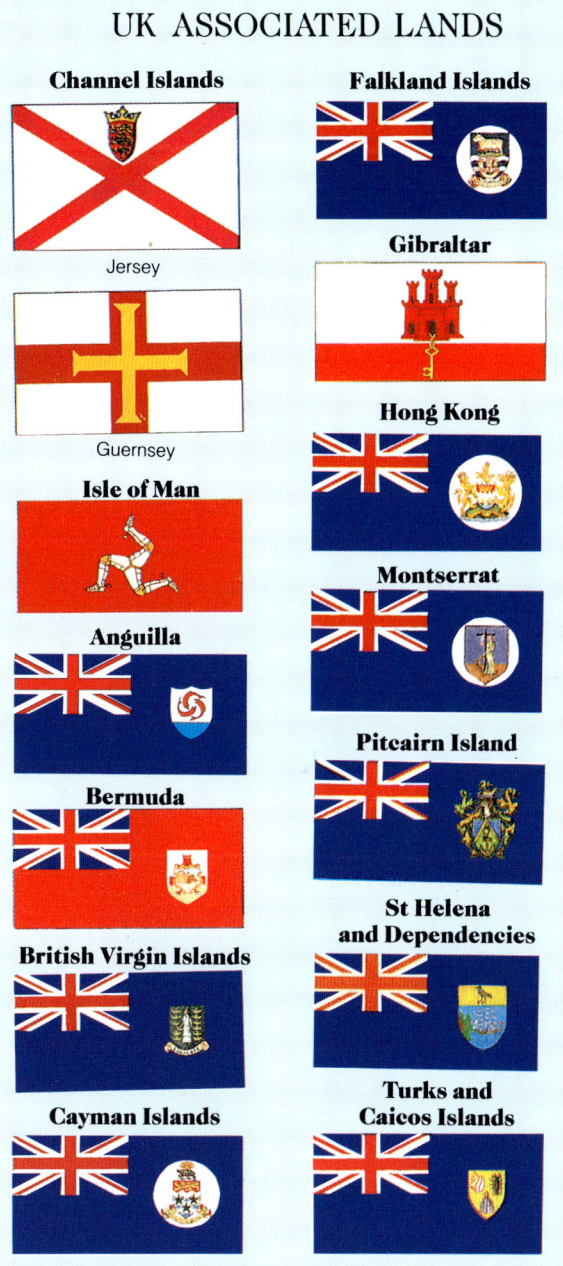

UK ASSOCIATED LANDS

Channel Islands

Jersey

Guernsey

Isle of Man

Anguilla

Bermuda

British Virgin Islands

Cayman Islands

Falkland Islands

Gibraltar

Hong Kong

Montserrat

Pitcairn Island

St Helena and Dependencies

Turks and Caicos Islands

UNITED STATES OF AMERICA

POPULATIOIN 247,100,000
CAPITAL: Washington D.C.
AREA: 3,620,000 sq mi (9,375,000 km^2)
LANGUAGES: English, numerous others
RELIGION: Christianity (Jewish and Islamic minorities)

Possibly the most famous flag in the world, the Stars and Stripes (known also as Old Glory and as the Star-Spangled Banner) has a field of 13 alternating stripes of red and white (seven red, six white), representing the 13 original states, and a blue canton containing 50 stars, representing the 50 States of the Union. The original version of the flag was adopted on 14 June 1777, replacing a variety of revolutionary flags including the Grand Union Flag (or Continental Colours), first raised at the beginning of 1776 by George Washington (1732–99) in proclaiming the organization of the Continental Army; this flag had the 13 stripes but a Union Jack in the canton. Between 1795 and 1818 the number of both stripes and stars was 15, acknowledging the admission of Vermont and Kentucky; in 1818, however, Congress determined that in future the number of stripes should be restricted to 13 – but that a new star should be added to recognize each new state on the 4 July succeeding its admission. The origins of the Stars and Stripes' design are obscure, only later did sentimentality give rise to popular and usually fallacious explanations. By far the most popular story concerns Elizabeth (Betsy) Ross (1752–1836), a flagmaker of Philadelphia. Her grandson, William J. Canby, basing his story on family traditions, from 1870 claimed that she was asked in June 1776 by a committee of Congress (including Washington himself) to stitch the first Stars and Stripes from a sketch they supplied to her. However, there is no record of Congress having made any decisions concerning the independence flag before 1777 and, while examples are not unknown, it seems unlikely that a symbol of independence would be commissioned so far in advance of the declaration of that independence. Another and more plausible claim is that of Francis Hopkinson (1737–91), a signatory of the Declaration of Independence, who in 1780 billed Congress for having designed the flag. Although Congress declined to pay his

The arms of the USA

bill on the grounds that many people had contributed to the design, it did not straightforwardly rebut his claim.

The law of 1818 stipulating the number of stripes and the timing of addition of future stars provided only a general description of the flag, and various versions were created over the years. Precise colours varied, but more importantly so did the arrangement of the stars – they were usually in rows but could be in a circle or arranged to form a larger star; during the American Civil War the stars were often in gold rather than white. Not until 1912 was the design officially standardized (with revisions in 1959 and 1960 to accommodate Alaska and Hawaii, respectively). In 1942 Congress brought into law a precise code of etiquette for use in conjunction with the flag governing such practices as the speed of its raising and lowering and its display on or near every schoolhouse on schooldays. In 1953 this code was amended to permit the UN flag to be flown above the Stars and Stripes.

It was the flag with 15 stars and 15 stripes that during the War of 1812 was flying over Fort McHenry in Baltimore Harbor on the night of 13 September 1813 and inspired Francis Scott Key (1779–1843) to write "The Star-Spangled Banner", which in 1931 by Act of Congress became the US national anthem.

USA – STATES OF THE UNION

Alabama

Arkansas

Connecticut

Alaska

California

Delaware

Arizona

Colorado

Florida

USA – STATES OF THE UNION

Georgia

Iowa

Maryland

Hawaii

Kansas

Massachusetts

Idaho

Kentucky

Michigan

Illinois

Louisiana

Minnesota

Indiana

Maine

Mississippi

USA – STATES OF THE UNION

Missouri

New Jersey

Ohio

Montana

New Mexico

Oklahoma

Nebraska

New York

Oregon

Nevada

North Carolina

Pennsylvania

New Hampshire

North Dakota

Rhode Island

USA – STATES OF THE UNION

South Carolina

Virginia

South Dakota

Washington

Tennessee

West Virginia

Texas

Wisconsin

Utah

Wyoming

Vermont

District of Columbia

USA ASSOCIATED LANDS

American Samoa

Guam

Midway Island
Uses the US flag

Virgin Islands of the United States

Wake Island

URUGUAY
The Oriental Republic of Uruguay

In 1828, on gaining independence (with UK and Argentine help) not only from its traditional Spanish overlords but also from Brazil, which had opportunistically invaded in 1820, Uruguay wished to use for its flag the same liberation colours as Argentina (*q.v.*) as well as the revolutionary symbol of the Sun of May. The model chosen for the new flag was the Stars and Stripes of the United States of America (*q.v.*), which had gained its own independence only some 50 years earlier. The nine alternate stripes of blue and white represent the nine original departments of Uruguay. The flag of 1828 was adapted into its current form in 1830; since then the details of the solar image have from time to time been revised.

POPULATION: 3,060,000
CAPITAL: Montevideo
AREA: 68,500 sq mi (177,500 km^2)
LANGUAGE: Spanish
RELIGION: Christianity (mainly RC)

UZBEKISTAN
The Republic of Uzbekistan

Uzbekistan has been a unitary state since 1991, having become so at the time of the general dissolution of the Union of Soviet Socialist Republics. It gained its name from Khan Uzbek (1312–42), one of the Golden Horde of Tatar warriors that terrorized and conquered much of Asia and eastern Europe during the 13th century. By the 16th century the Uzbek people had come to dominate the region, and in the late 19th century Uzbekistan became Russian; in 1924 it was established as the Uzbek SSR. Uzbekistan's flag was adopted in 1991. The blue is said to recall the flag of Tamerlane, while the new moon stands for rebirth and the stars remind us that astronomy and astrology were developed in medieval Uzbekistan.

POPULATION: 17,990,000
CAPITAL: Taskent (Tashkent)
AREA: 172,800 sq mi (447,600 km^2)
LANGUAGES: Turkic languages
RELIGION: Islam

VANUATU
The Republic of Vanuatu

On a map the islands that form Vanuatu form a rough Y, and this shape is overt in the flag adopted a few months before the republic gained its independence in 1980. Within the angle of the Y is a boar's tusk, a native emblem of plenty; within the tusk are two leaves of a local fern (*namele*), which symbolizes peace; their 39 fronds represent the 39 members of the nation's legislative assembly.

POPULATION: 150,000
CAPITAL: Port-Vila
AREA: 5,700 sq mi (14,760 km^2)
LANGUAGES: Pidgin English, French, indigenous languages
RELIGIONS: Christianity (mainly Protestant), indigenous religions

POPULATION: 770
AREA: 0.17 sq mi (0.44 km^2)
LANGUAGES: Latin, Italian
RELIGION: Christianity (RC)

VATICAN CITY
Vatican City State

The Vatican City State was created in 1929, and the flag it adopted then has remained unchanged. Based on a merchant flag used by the Papal States from 1825 to 1870, it shows, beneath the papal triple crown, an image of the keys referred to in *Matthew, xvi,* 18–19: "And I say also unto thee, That thou art Peter, and upon this rock I will build my church . . . And I will give unto thee the keys of the kingdom of heaven: and whatsoever thou shalt bind on earth shalt be bound in heaven: and whatsoever thou shalt loose on earth shall be loosed in heaven." The keys are gold and silver, representing binding and loosing; the red cord tying the keys shows that these powers operate together. The background reflects the colours of the keys.

POPULATION: 18,750,000
CAPITAL: Caracas
AREA: 352,000 sq mi (912,000 km^2)
LANGUAGE: Spanish
RELIGION: Christianity (almost exclusively RC)

VENEZUELA
The Republic of Venezuela

The flag of Venezuela is similar to those of Ecuador and Colombia (*qq.v.*) (see Columbia text). The yellow, blue and red colours of all three were those adopted by the Venezuelan freedom fighter Francisco de Miranda (1750–1816) to convey the nation (yellow) was separated by the sea (blue) from Spain, the red seemingly indicating both liberation and the blood of their people. The current version of the Venezuelan flag was adopted in 1954. The seven stars represent the seven provinces of Venezuela liberated by de Miranda in 1811. The complicated national arms – white horse, wheatsheaf, battle-colours, etc – have a likewise complicated scroll beneath them whose legend has varied according to the political climes.

POPULATION: 64,200,000
CAPITAL: Hanoi
AREA: 127,000 sq mi (330,000 km^2)
LANGUAGES: Vietnamese, Chinese, French, English
RELIGION: Buddhism (Christian minority)

VIETNAM
The Socialist Republic of Vietnam

A form of the modern Vietnamese flag was used by the soldiers of Ho Chi Minh (1892–1969) in their struggle against the Japanese during World War II. The Japanese expelled, the struggle of Ho Chi Minh's freedom fighters was now directed against the colonial French; his communist troops continued to fly the red flag with a yellow star, which had the usual socialist meanings. In 1954 the French were ousted, and the Geneva Conference established the communist North Vietnam and the supposedly democratic South Vietnam. The North continued to use Ho Chi Minh's flag, revising it slightly in 1955. Civil war between the two states continued until 1975, when the North subsumed the South and adopted the 1955 flag for the whole country.

WESTERN SAMOA
The Independent State of Western Samoa

Independence came to Western Samoa in 1962 for the second time; the first had been in 1889, under King Malietoa Laupepa. When he died in 1898, the islands came under the control of Germany, with UK and US agreement. Following World War I New Zealand annexed the islands in 1919, administering them until the second independence, although they were self-governing from 1959. The New Zealand influence is evident in the use of the Southern Cross in the Western Samoan flag, which was established with four stars (as in the New Zealand flag) in 1948 and revised to its modern form, with the additional smaller star, in 1949. The red comes from King Malietoa Laupepa's flag, and the blue from the New Zealand flag.

POPULATION: 167,000
CAPITAL: Apia
AREA: 1,100 sq mi (2,840 km^2)
LANGUAGES: Samoan, English
RELIGION: Christianity

YEMEN
The Republic of Yemen

Until 22 May 1990 there were two Yemens, North Yemen (or the Yemen Arab Republic) and the larger although less populous South Yemen (or the People's Democratic Republic of Yemen). Until 1990 North Yemen's had been in the Pan-Arab colours shared by Jordan (*q.v.*) and others, but arranged as in that of Syria (*q.v.*), with whom Egypt and North Yemen had formed the United Arab Republic between 1958 and 1961; the North Yemeni flag had a single, five-pointed green star (representing Arab unity) in the central white band. The South Yemeni flag had been essentially a similar tricolour but without the green star and with the superimposition at left of a blue triangle containing a red, nationalist five-pointed star. Today's flag is the simple tricolour.

POPULATION: 11,110,000
CAPITAL: San'a
AREA: 207,400 sq mi (531,900 km^2)
LANGUAGES: Arabic, English
RELIGION: Islam

YUGOSLAVIA
The Federal Republic of Yugoslavia

Until 1991/2 Yugoslavia contained as republics what have now become three independent nations; Croatia, Slovenia and Bosnia and Herzegovina. Currently there still remain within Yugoslavia three constituent republics. Yugoslavia's history is short. It was formed by the federation of Bosnia and Herzegovina, Croatia, Macedonia, Montenegro, Serbia and Slovenia, gaining its modern name in 1927. The communist star at the centre of the flag was adopted in 1946 and dropped in 1992; the coloured stripes, representing pan-Slav unity, date from the country's formation in 1918.

POPULATION: 17,106,700
CAPITAL: Belgrade (Beograd)
AREA: 99,000 sq mi (256,000 km^2)
LANGUAGES: Serbo-Croat, Macedonian, Albanian, others
RELIGIONS: Christianity, Islam

ZAIRE
The Republic of Zaire

Formerly the Belgian Congo, Zaïre has not enjoyed a tranquil history since attaining independence in 1960. Established at first as the Republic of the Congo, it suffered anarchy within days. Since 1965, Joseph Mobutu has ruled over a virtual dictatorship. In 1971 Mobutu declared the country a one-party state, with himself as leader of this one party, the MPR (*Mouvement Populaire de la Révolution*) and hence automatically national president; the name of the nation was changed to Zaïre, and a new national flag – almost identical with that of the MPR – introduced. The flag is in the Pan-African red, yellow and green, with their usual meanings; the torch represents liberty and the struggle for it.

POPULATION: 34,000,000
CAPITAL: Kinshasa
AREA: 905,600 sq mi (2,345,500 km²)
LANGUAGES: French, Lingala, Swahili, Kikongo, Tshiluba
RELIGIONS: indigenous religions, Christianity (Islamic minority)

ZAMBIA
The Republic of Zambia

When Zambia attained independence in 1964 its first ruling party was the United National Independence Party, led by Kenneth Kaunda (1924–), and this circumstance has obtained ever since, the UNIP being legally confirmed as the country's sole political party in 1972. The colours of the Zambian flag are those that the UNIP claimed for its own in 1964, and the flag has remained unchanged since then even though those of the UNIP have altered. The green background is for the country's agriculture and forestry, the black for its people and the red for the usual progressive sentiments; the curious orangey colour of the third strip reflects the importance of copper in the nation's economy. The eagle signifies the desire for freedom.

POPULATION: 7,530,000
CAPITAL: Lusaka
AREA: 291,000 sq mi (753,000 km²)
LANGUAGES: English, Bemba, Nyanja and many others
RELIGIONS: Christianity, indigenous religions

ZIMBABWE
The Republic of Zimbabwe

The current flag of Zimbabwe was introduced with the declaration of the new republic in 1980, the black central stripe (reflecting the colour of the country's majority) and the Pan-African colours being taken straight from the flag of ZANU (Zimbabwe African National Union), which had been the majority grouping among the forces struggling for majority rule. The black-rimmed white triangle was introduced to symbolize the country's new black rulers' desire for cooperation and peace with the white minority – a laudable generosity of spirit in view of the nation's history. The five-pointed red star stands for internationalism. The soapstone bird is an emblem associated with the ancient ruined city of Zimbabwe, from which the republic drew its name.

POPULATION: 8,900,000
CAPITAL: Harare
AREA: 151,000 sq mi (391,000 km²)
LANGUAGES: English, Shona, Ndebele
RELIGIONS: Christianity, indigenous religions (Islamic minority)

Africa

Europe

Eurasia